AGE-GROUP SWIMMING

A clinic to help Age-Group in Jamaica. Mrs Dawson used a Christmas holiday to train her own swimmers with the Jamaicans in Kingston in 1962. Here Mrs Dawson, daughter of the famous United States swimming coach, Matt Mann, demonstrates stroke technique at the Olympic Pool of the University College of the West Indies, a branch of the University of London at Kingston

ROSE MARY DAWSON

Age-Group
Swimming

A BLUEPRINT
FOR OLYMPIC SUCCESS

The great exposure programme for American
children may be a key to fitness, happiness,
and Olympic success in swimming, as well
as other sports and in other lands

PELHAM BOOKS

First published in Great Britain by
PELHAM BOOKS LTD
26 Bloomsbury Street
London, W.C.1
1965

© 1965 by Rose Mary Dawson

Set and printed in Great Britain by Tonbridge Printers Ltd,
Peach Hall Works, Tonbridge, Kent, in Baskerville eleven on
twelve point, on paper made by Henry Bruce at Currie,
Midlothian, and bound by James Burn at Esher, Surrey

To My Father
MATT MANN
who travelled all the
swimming trails before me

Introduction

by Adolph Kiefer

My friends all kid me about my business street address, not wrong side of the tracks jokes like I used to get when I was on Railroad Avenue, but patriotic jokes because my new street number is 1775.

'Adolph,' they say, 'What comes after 1775?'

'1776?'

'That's the spirit, Adolph!'

This old joke refers to the spirit of '76, theme of the American Revolution, only my business is swimming so my street address should be 1953, the first big year of a thing called Age-Group, the American Revolution in swimming. This revolution, which has since swept through the swimming world, came after Carl Bauer's manifesto at the 1949 AAV Convention and after Beth Kaufman's California trial in 1952. Bauer and Kaufman are the father and mother of age-group swimming and their offspring has been like the Genie who got out of the bottle. As Rose Mary Dawson points out in this fine new book, the problem is not how to make Age-Group grow but how to control that growth in the best interest of all swimming. Certainly, we all must agree that age-group is responsible for the American Olympic success; the question is how to make it more responsible. This has required constant adjustments and rule changes, but basicly age-group is sound in health and some form of this age-regulated youth programme can be adapted to other sports and other countries. If you have not started your programme, please read this book before you do start.

I never thought about it too much before reading the manuscript for this book, but the percentages that exist in any competitive sport are all against the parent who expects any one son or daughter to grow into an athletic champion. Even with horses, carefully bred and trained for certain champion qualities, there is slim chance that any one horse will be *the* horse that grows up to win the big races. With humans the variables are so much greater that no one parent should expect to have a

7

champion even after one is well on the way. Raising a champion swimmer is a blessing, not a birthright. You cannot will, wish or push a child to glory although you must back him and push just a bit until the boy or girl reaches an age for self-motivated unconditional commitment. Too much early push will kill this initiative when the point is reached where you cannot swim the race for him and too little push will not get him ready for his opportunity when it comes. If your child has the talent you have a responsibility and an obligation but apparently not a right to expectation.

The world is full of coaches and former athletes who understand this delicate paradox, coaches and ex-athletes who want the same for their children, yet it is a rare occasion when a coach's son reaches stardom and the bygone champion almost never gets to relive his dreams with another generation. I am fortunate to have had two sons who made it.

Matt Mann was also very fortunate. This all-time great swim coach had a son who became a national champion but even with such an ideal environment, a tremendous desire to please his Dad and willingness to be coached by a master, this chip-off-the-old-block did everything right but did not have that rare combination of good luck and the many other things it takes to make an Olympic team. Matt Mann, Jr., missed by $\frac{1}{5}$ second. We age-group parents must understand, above all else, that many are chosen but few are called. The parent with one swimmer must understand the mathematics of swimming, as does the coach with 100 swimmers. The chances are against any one swimmer and this is what makes the competition.

Matt Mann's daughter, the author of this book, never really tried as a competitive swimmer. Her father was a men's coach and without a girl's team to swim for she was not really interested. On infrequent practice she swam excellent times for her age, but anyone saying she would have made it or even she could have made it is only speculating. There are always more excuses than champions. Now that Matt Mann's daughter is Coach Rose Mary Dawson there is no longer any need for speculation or excuse. She has found her part of her father's dream. Many say she's the old man's daughter when they see her coach. She has his lungs and she has his touch. She is successful but she also knows better than most, that success is only

8

10 per cent inspiration and 90 per cent perspiration – even when coaching swimmers with 100 per cent talent. This is why she says, and I reiterate that the success of the American Age-Group Swimming programme owes its greatest success, first, last and always to numbers.

Sure, age-group has started the swimmers younger which is probably a good thing, and sure, age-group has provided standards of measured achievement and hard work, spread public interest and established rules, but its biggest contribution is more children swimming in more pools for more coaches, a competitive situation that is the law of the land.

Before 1953 we had some good American swimmers, but only in isolated areas. Hawaii, Australia, Scotland, England, Denmark, France and Holland also had isolated areas, perhaps better isolated areas than ours, and at least the results were competitive. The Americans also had some great coaches but they were few and they did not communicate with each other, in fact, most of them guarded their trade secrets.

A book such as this probably would never have been published in my time as a swimmer – which was a long period (12 years) by present laws of attrition. I was fortunate to grow up in one of the good swimming areas and to have good coaching, but how many, like me, or not like me, never knew and will never know whether they have Adolph Kiefer's swimming talent? This situation is still the case in most areas of the world where swimming is a minor sport or a major sport confined to isolated areas with a good club, a good coach and a good pool, in that order. This is still the case most places, but not in the United States where age-group swimming and resulting public enthusiasm has increased the number of swimclubs, the number of knowledgeable coaches and the number of swimmers a hundredfold. With 500,000 swimmers, well coached and trained in a good national programme, everybody's children who have the desire, can give it a try and since more are trying, more will succeed even at 100 to 1 odds, odds getting greater and swimming more competitive as the numbers of competitors grows.

Age-Group swimming has greatly improved the quality of the U.S. Olympic Swimming team but it has also decreased the chances of any one parent's swimmer making the team. The

9

sport is bigger and its influence greater, but chance of reaching the top is slimmer. This may not be for you but so long as the Americans have this great exposure programme and no one else has it, just so long will the U.S.A. have most of the Olympic champions in swimming. To win, other countries must keep up with the times and must introduce age-group or something like it. If a parent, a coach or the swimming association of any country will accept the law of percentage and get with mass exposure, then age-group will work for you. Rose Mary Dawson's book spells out how it will work and how it has already worked in the U.S.A.

Sometimes I am glad and sometimes I am sad that we did not have age-group when I was a swimmer in the 1930s and early '40s. My times would have been faster and my records might look better by today's standards, but I certainly would have had to work harder and I might not have lasted so long. In fact, or maybe its fancy, with so much competition I might not have made it at all. I was undefeated for 12 years and won an Olympic gold medal, but my son Dale, who is neither an Olympian nor undefeated, has beat my times in every stroke. Whoever knows who is greater, father or son? The point here is not a comparison with the good old days but the blunt fact that a nation cannot do it any more without age-group swimming.

AUTHOR'S NOTE: I would cringe to hear most of the little age-groupers say 'But Mum, who is Adolph Kiefer?', so, swimming fame being as unstable as last year's time standards, I will introduce my introducer. Adolph Kiefer is the father of four age-group swimmers, two boys and two girls. The two boys are now swimming for Yale University. Adolph is president of the Adolph Kiefer Co., who's motto is 'We manufacture everything but the water'. He ranks second to Weismuller on most everybody's list of all-time American greats and by any standards that last, he must be rated as the World's all-time greatest backstroker. He held all world records for backstroke for *15* years and the individual medley records off and on for many years. He lost only one backstroke race in his entire life. That was in world record time to Harry Holliday. Adolph went to work and the next time out, he got his record back.

He did not lose a swimming race for 8 years. When he won the backstroke race at the 1936 Berlin Olympics he is supposed to have had time to wipe his nose as he went by Hitler's box. He will not confirm this story. Kiefer is also modest in a strange sort of fashion. He was bitten by a Japanese monkey while touring Bepo at the last Olympics. Back in Tokyo a woman asked him if he was as great a swimmer as Tarzan Johnny Weissmuller. 'No, lady,' said Kiefer, rolling up his sleeve to show an ugly sore, 'a monkey would never bite Weismuller.'

Illustrations

A clinic to help Age-Group in Jamaica   *frontispiece*

An inexpensive bulkhead pool at Mrs Dawson's
camp   *facing page* 40

Swim champions Suzy Thrasher (U.S.) and Sara
Barber (Canada)   40

The late Matt Mann coached children at his
daughter's camp   41

Suzy Thrasher   56

Marty Sinn, world's professional marathon record-
holder   57

Camp Chicopi   64

Breast-stroke champions Bonnie Benson (Canada) and
Susan Rogers (U.S.)   64

Mrs Dawson's daughter, Marilyn   65

Mrs Dawson and her husband, Buck   96

Bumpy Jones, 1952 Olympic team   97

Swimmers from U.S., Canada, Mexico and Puerto
Rico   104

Florida Christmas reunion   104

Age-group swimmers in Australia   105

Young age-group swimmers at Camp Ab-O-Mak   105

Age-group swimmers from New England   120

This trio won National AAU medley relay title   120

Mrs Dawson packing   121

Trampoline exercises   136

Two studies of a very young age-grouper   137

The Puerto Rico Swimming Association team   152

Games help to kep age-group swimmers active   153

Contents

Introduction by Adolph Kiefer   7

1   A Lesson from the Tokyo Olympics   15

2   Why a Book on Age-Group Swimming?   19

3   The Age-Group Founders Talk About Their Brain-Child (Carl Bauer and Beth Kaufman – the first age-group parents)   26

4   Towards a Better Philosophy in Age-Group Swimming   32

5   Where Age-Group may be Failing Us   36

6   The Structure of Age-Group Swimming   42

7   Organising an Age-Group Swim Club   47

8   Age-Group Training. Is it Different?   49

9   Age-Group Diving   53

10   Junior Olympics and Other Age Plans   59

11   The Age-Group Parent – Jekyll or Hyde?   63

12   How Various Coaches Handle Parents – The Percentage of Success – Teaching or Training and Other Matters   68

13   A Dozen Do's and Don't's on Meet Behaviour for Age-Group Parents   72

14   Operation Mexico (The U.S.A. needs a National Age-Group Contest)   74

15   A Bit of Age-Group Swimming History   78

16   Why Your Daughter Should Swim   97

17   Michigan's Development League – An Autumn Plan for Swimming   101

18   One Other Way to Keep Our Children from Quitting   105

19   Towards a Better Philosophy in American Women's Physical Education   107

13

20 Bringing Up Father. (Carlos Sala of Puerto Rico
    gives His Philosophy on Age-Group Swimming)   112

21 Age-Group Swimming in Britain by W. J. Juba,
    Assistant Editor of the *Swimming Times*   115

22 Age-Group Swimming in Australia and Holland
    by Forbes Carlile (Former Australian and Dutch
    National coach)   119

23 Age-Group Testimonials from Parents, Doctors and
    Swimming Writers   126

Appendix I Official U.S. AAU Age-Group Swimming
    and Diving Rules   151

Appendix II Conversion of metres to yards and feet 158

1

A Lesson from the Tokyo Olympics

At the Tokyo Olympics 66 per cent of all swimming medals were won by one country, the United States of America. This included 37 out of 56 swim medals, 9 of 12 diving medals, and all gold medals in relays. This remarkable showing, according to U.S. Olympic Men's Coach Jim Counsilman and U.S. Olympic Women's Coach Peter Deland, must be attributed to age-group swimming. Every one of the U.S. swimmers was a graduate, or a current undergraduate, of the U.S. AAU Age-Group Swimming Programme.

Quoting from the Japanese newspaper *The Mainichi News*: 'The greatest sensation of the Olympics is the record-shattering performances of United States teenagers.' In a world of teenagers fighting for identity, this seems to be the best way to compete in an adult world because it is teenagers competing and winning in something measured against all ages by age-old standards of excellence. Measured sports performances cannot be discredited by the experience of another generation as can teenage music or almost any other teen accomplishment.

As a matter of fact, the shortcomings in U.S. Olympic performance must be attributed to adults and not teenagers, the philosophy of educators, who are against competition, especially women's physical educators who persist in the view that competition is harmful to girls and children. This attitude erodes the desire necessary for competitive excellence. Instead of mass exposure, as in age-group swimming, we get only isolated islands of interest in other sports. Even in swimming, it is rare to get institutional backing since most women's physical educators are indoctrinated to battle against competition. As the man said in *The Mainichi News*, 'it's a teenage world' and few adults have the confidence to tell the school administrators they are wrong. Athletic directors will not fight to add girls' sports unless there is parent pressure to do so. Why? Too much

15

work and their own lady gym teachers are against it. We are in a competitive society. Educators opposed to competition in sport seem strangely socialistic. The argument about hurting children with Varsity sports catering to the few can quickly be solved by having more Varsity sports, a team for everybody willing to strive for accomplishment and recognition. Varsity, and not intramural, is the key to greater interest. We need more Varsities to inspire more children.

We need Olympic Champions and Varsity sports for stimulation and inspiration as an incentive for mass fitness programmes. I am sympathetic with those of us who wish to improve Olympic records as an international symbol of strength and I am in sympathy with those who decry our lack of youth fitness and wish it for better physical health. Both these arguments can stand alone as worthwhile causes but they are inalterably coupled. An improvement in our Olympic image will encourage fitness, and an improvement in fitness, and fitness programmes will supply material for our Olympic programmes.

The major problem in our society is neither fitness nor Olympic prestige however, but the desire of teenagers to find outlets in which they can produce some kind of quick results, individual recognition in a population explosion which has decreased the influence of any single person. Riots are one answer, a full-scale programme of competitive sports for all would be a much better answer. This programme would feed the fitness programme some of us want and the Olympic potentials some of us want. The Olympic Champions and the physically fit would inspire participation. The programme goes both ways. How can we possibly find fault with it? The question is, why not? Why not insist that our educators give us a sensible answer on their objections to competitive sports in our competitive society.

Many Olympic coaches went back to their homelands after Tokyo to instigate a programme similar to our age-group swimming. Many of our own coaches in other sports want to do likewise, but it is not as simple as it looks. Age-group swimming has worked as a mass exposure programme (and not too mass) because of parents who would fight bureaucracy. When school administrations and recreation departments refused to have a comprehensive competitive programme, these parents organized on a private club basis and used money to build a private pool,

16

or pressure to get into a public pool. These kinds of parents are not too common in any one community and most of those with guts enough, interest enough, and self-confidence in their cause have already stood up to be counted. Similar age-group programmes in other sports will offer these few parents more options for their children but it will not increase proportionately the total numbers of children involved in age-group competitive sports programmes. This can only come by changing the attitude of educators and recreation people, particularly women, so that we get institutional backing for our exposure programmes. Only then will we have a majority, or even a sizeable and healthy minority, of our children involved in competitive age-group sports programmes.

U.S. teenage boy swimmers were the talk of the Tokyo Olympics just as U.S. teenage girls stole the 'ows' and 'ahs' in Rome. Boys are not supposed to mature as fast, but Nelson was still 16, Schollander 18, Anderson 19, plus others still in their teens.

Many a foreign coach asked us how our middle-teen girls and late-teen boys can whip their mature athletes. We tried to explain that our amateurs nearly all quit before they get to the age of athletic maturity so we use the best we have from a very large and young lot. This may sound like an argument for our teenage girls quitting young before even younger teenage girls push by them, but it is not. I would still like to see what our Von Saltza's and de Verona's could do if they'd stay interested as long as Australia's Dawn Fraser has remained in competitive swimming.

Quoting from Dr James Counsilman, the U.S. Olympic coach: 'America has been the No. 1 swimming country, not because we are approaching our swimming more scientifically, nor because we have trained more intelligently, nor that we know more about the fluid mechanics of swimming. We owe our success to two factors – our large number of swimming-pools and the large number of competitors engaged in the sport – primarily age-group swimmers. We probably have more pools than the rest of the countries of the world put together; the same thing may be said for the number of competitive swimmers.'

Dr Counsilman might also have added that the U.S.A. has more professional coaches than the rest of the world combined,

17

not necessarily better coaches but more coaches. In any swimming success story we must first acknowledge that swimmers go and grow where the coaches are.

My father, the late Matt Mann, was English born but most of his coaching career was spent in the United States. It took him 50 years of coaching in the U.S.A. to get used to the idea that he was being paid to do what he would have wanted to do anyway, even without pay. Contrary to my father's counting his blessings however, the idea that coaches as well as swimmers should be amateurs is abhorrent to the American concept, and this is why the U.S. attracts so many good people into coaching. The U.S. coach does not regard his coaching as a hobby, nor could he afford to do so. Coaching is his profession, and it is a respected profession. Most U.S. coaches have age-group teams and learn-to-swim classes in addition to college or high school coaching jobs, life-saving, and teaching. They work long dedicated hours, often many more than their job demands, but they always regard themselves as professional coaches. They stand on their record as coaches, work long hours as coaches, draw their pay as coaches, and do as little besides coaching as possible. These proud and dedicated professionals control their own destinies in swimming and they control most U.S. swimming. They are predominately college graduates, articulate, and well educated. The quality of the American coach and the system which allows him professional status have a great deal to do with U.S. swimming success. Only by raising the professional status of swim coaches throughout the world can we hope to attract large numbers of hard working full-time coaches in other countries. The professional age-group coach is another keystone of American Age-Group success.

2

Why a Book on Age-Group Swimming?

Since American teen-age swimming performances were the sensation of Tokyo, and since question after question asked 'how come?' and the answer was always the same, 'Age-Group', there will be a tendency for other countries* and other sports to imitate the American age-group swimming programme. The purpose of this book is to cover every aspect of that programme, its history, its growing pains, its past, present, and future problems.

Basically, any programme must fit into the way of life, the philosophy, and the social structure of the country involved. The U.S. is a large country, and age-group involves large numbers of children, but it is not a representative programme and the people in less populous countries should consider this before imitating the programme. Sports in the United States are organized in and through the schools and school-dominated recreation departments. There are very few athletes beyond college age except in professional sports. Swimming is not a professional sport and top-flight swimming requires too much training-time to fit the American business way of life which requires a man to go out and earn a living as soon as he graduates from college. Except for the Armed Forces, the U.S. has few mature amateur athletes in professions which will allow them time to train.

At the other end of the scale, Americans begin school at 5, and school from ages 5 to 22 is a nine-months-of-the-year proposition, therefore successful sports programmes must be school-oriented. The exception is the summer vacation period, three months during which sports are not school-oriented but are dominated by recreation departments using school facilities. These recreation departments are school-oriented and often

* See chapter 20 by W. J. Juba

under the control of the board of education. All such recreation and school programmes are local, and state or province organized, legislated, and controlled, as opposed to national programmes. This conforms to the U.S. tradition that education should be city and state controlled, not national. Let's keep this educational influence in mind as we review the traditions of U.S. swimming as opposed to most other sports.

The United States, with a few lapses, has been the dominant world swimming power since 1920. Swimming came first in the downtown athletic clubs in major cities. These clubs took special swimming talent found in the YMCA's and the Hawaiian Islands, subsidized this talent to compete in the name of the club, and hired the best available coach to help bring the talent along. Bachrach, Cody, Mann, Pinkston, and Daughters, were among the great American coaches who worked these clubs. A few clubs had all the top swimmers, and these swimmers had jobs through club members who allowed them time to train and travel when necessary. These swimmers were the giants of their day, Kahanamoko, Ross, Weismuller, Crabbe, and Kiefer, plus Arne Borg when he was in the United States.

By 1928 a few college boys began to show up on the Olympic team. There were a few more in 1932. 1936 was about half college, and the post-war 1948 and 1952 teams were all college men. Many of the world's best swimmers from other lands were also trained in American colleges; Davies, Marshall, and Aubry, from Australia, Ford from Panama, the Wardrops from Scotland, Duncan, Johnson, Meirims, Steurt from South Africa and Hurring from New Zealand.

American teams won most of the Olympic swimming medals although a very young school-oriented Japanese swimming programme shared honours in 1932 and 1936, actually winning more swim medals but losing overall because of American domination in diving.

The year of reckoning came in 1956 when the American college swimmers, and the many foreign swimmers training in U.S. colleges, went down the drain before a group of summer-trained Australians who had trained harder than it was believed a man can do and still get his studies in college. These Australians set the modern standards of hard training and resulting swimming excellence. In 1952 they had won one gold medal with American-trained John Davies. By 1956 they won almost everything with their own training.

1956 also marked the end of the Hawaiian era. Since 1912 American Olympic teams, and Olympic Games swimming in general, had usually been dominated by swimmers from the tiny Hawaiian Islands where swimming was part of the way of life, just as long-distance running had been part of a Scandinavian way of life. The six Hawaiians on the 1956 U.S. Olympic team were the last. It marked the end of an era.

It also marked the end of the era of college domination of U.S. Olympic swimming, although the colleges did not know it then. Colleges with the American emphasis on college athletics (with or without athletic scholarships), still play a major role in keeping boys in swimming four years after high school. Outstanding college coaches also advance the swimmers' technique, often ignored in age-group swimming, but the colleges are no longer the major factor in *training* top-level swimmers. This role has gone back to the clubs, but not the same kind of clubs as the downtown athletic clubs of the '20's and early '30's. The new club is a group of parents, and a coach renting time in a municipal swimming-pool.

Today's U.S. Olympic swimmers come out of an age-group swimming programme begun as recently as 1953. It began as a way to overcome the abuses of an unsatisfactory novice swimming classification. The genie got out of the bottle. Age-group was an instant success. It got a great many children into swimming. Age-group is first, last, and always, a mass exposure programme, perhaps the most mass exposure programme in the history of any Olympic sport, although Russian weightlifters may have a counter-claim on total numbers. There were more than 500,000 registered AAU age-group swimmers by 1964, and the Olympic trials looked like togetherness with not one but ten or more world-class competitors vying for each spot on the Olympic team. The Americans took five boys and five girl breast-strokers, butterflyers, back-strokers and enough free-stylers so that they had 'B' qualification relays breaking world records in the preliminaries, and a totally different set of 'A' swimmers in the relay finals. Frequently, a great swimmer from another country at the Olympics would look across the starting blocks and find herself bracketed by Americans. There was

21

another American team at home, Olympic trials losers, a team which might well have finished second to their countrymen in Tokyo.

There were great individual performances by swimmers from other countries, of course, but the psychological advantage and the great depth of talent belonged to the Americans with two or three in most finals. 'Why?' 'Age-Group Swimming!' The Americans never had such depth before age-group swimming.

So, every other sport, and every other country, should run out and get an age-group programme? Perhaps, but the results may not be quite the same. The United States did have the tradition of top Olympic swimming before age-group. The pools were there and so were the coaches, although not in such numbers. Age-group has been an exposure programme to more children than ever swam competitively before but it is more of a feeder programme than a developer of champions. The best age-group programmes of meets and administration are in Illinois, Michigan, and Ontario, yet these states and province very rarely produce a world-class girl swimmer. Why? Because the swimming in Illinois and Michigan has been high school oriented, and there are no high school teams for girls, and because swimming has never caught on in Ontario no matter how good the programme. The best coaches in Illinois are in men's high school swimming. They are in high school and college swimming in Michigan. Some of these men have age-group club teams using their high school or country club facilities, but these club teams are oriented to the interests of the coach, producing high school or college male swimmers. So these boy swimmers in many cases, and girl swimmers in most cases, must still go somewhere else to find the coaches interested in developing Olympic girl (or boy) swimmers and national champions.

Just as before, the good swimmers must usually gravitate to the good coach. Sending the boy away to a college with a good coach was and is easy. Moving the whole family so that an age-group swimmer can progress is more difficult. Transplanting a youngster in his teens without his parents is a tremendous social risk.

Only the daring and dedicated parent (some would say over-zealous, even foolhardy) would uproot himself and move his

22

family half-way across the country so his child could have good coaching. In the American society, where business success is the social premium, this takes real guts. It also takes guts of some sort or other to ship your swim-talented child off to live with strangers when you cannot move yourself and, to a lesser degree, it takes guts to oppose the lady gym teacher and the school principal in your home community when these authorities peep out from behind their educational immunities and say 'your child is swimming too much'. The traditional view of American educators is opposed to any concentrated athletic programme 'overemphasis' and they are usually opposed to athletic competition of any kind for girls and children.

Since there are few children willing to depart from a school programme no matter how inadequate, and even fewer parents who will oppose the school, we must assume that age-group has gone about as far as it can until we get institutional backing. The mass popularity sports in the U.S.A. (football, basketball, baseball, athletics) are still school-oriented, as before. The same is true in Japan, and in many other countries. Most of the U.S. child-parent combinations willing to oppose the system are already in age-group swimming. There is competition from Little League baseball, football, and hockey. To expand age-group to include all the Olympic sports would give these rare parent-son, parent-daughter zealots more choice of sports, but it would not increase, proportionately, the number of participants. There might be more in age-group wrestling, and age-group track, but fewer in swimming, because all would come from the same small nucleus of children with parent backing, both willing to fight bureaucracy.

500,000 age-group swimmers are not really very many in a swim-conscious country the size of the U.S.A. and there will not be a great many more until we re-educate the educators, first to tolerate, and then to condone, and support, and finally to promote age-group sports with institutional backing, coaching, facilities, school honours. After we raise the status of our sport we will attract more of the sports-minded children into our sport.

Until then, age-group swimmers are just a remarkable fringe group of U.S. children backed by a fringe group of U.S. parents. They are a fierce independent group of rugged individuals, and from such come champions, but not nearly enough are participating with the sort of unconditional commitment that is needed to establish a sports-minded nation. So, the U.S. fringe group of 500,000 shrinks considerably when we seek quality and its demands on quantitative effort.

Japan, like the U.S., needs to upgrade its school attitude towards excellence in Olympic sport so long as that country, like the U.S., puts paramount importance on education, and so long as its amateur athletes must come either from school or from the armed forces. The Japanese first gave the world an indication of the hard work possible in swimming, and the youth possible in Olympic champions. This was in 1932 and 1936 but, somehow, their school programme has since lost both its quantitative and qualitative appeal. If and when the Japanese and the Americans demand that their schools take sports and fitness as seriously as maths and languages, we will be well on the way to a healthy age-group-type exposure programme for all, in all sports. This is even more important in a country like Japan where there is no long summer vacation to concentrate on academic-free sports interest.

If you can get the schools and the school coaches in your country to give you a strong programme, perhaps it should be by class grade (grade-group) rather than age-group. Some swim enthusiasts have even talked of weight group or height group since some children mature more rapidly than others. This has been tried, but not too successfully. The over-weight boy or girl who needs to swim is outclassed.

Another method is to hold A and B contests in age-group by setting qualifying times. This is a great improvement on the old novice idea because the stop-watch gives exact measure. The coaches and swim committee men sit down once a year and set up time standards for each stroke in each age and distance. Any swimmers meeting these standards are eligible for A class competition, ineligible for B, and *vice versa*. This system polices itself as contest results indicate the honesty or dishonesty of a coach who enters a swimmer in A before he is ready, or tries to cover up an A swimmer to win in B competition. This method is most successful in areas with a heavy swimming population and a desire to encourage swimmers at all levels and to encourage parents with shorter contests.

24

Smaller countries must work out their own solution to mass exposure and better development programmes just as each country has worked out its own peculiar definition of amateurism. Age-group mass exposure is not the only answer, as Jan Stender proved in 1955 with six world record-holders living on one street in Hilversum, Holland.

The Canadians, using virtually the same age-group system as the Americans, with a few improvements like open instead of 15–16–17, and a national telegraphic contest (see Chapter 12) nevertheless are not achieving the results, partly because they have only 3,000 registered swimmers instead of 500,000. Obviously, Canada with 3,000 should be more concerned with dropouts than the U.S.A. with 500,000. Age-group swimming in Canada is not the great exposure programme, and Australia, with a smaller population than Canada and a non age-group swim programme, has many times the swimmers, and many times the quality, of Canadian swimmers. Any Canadian taking exception to my remarks can truthfully say 'but the Australians have very little ice hockey, and hockey, not swimming, is our national sport'. Australia seems to be the world's greatest amateur sports country percentage of population-wise, but this is straying from the point which is age-group swimming.

The Americans have more coaches and more swimmers. They also have more better coaches, and more proficient swimmers, a competitive situation for which age-group is at least partly responsible. The United States also has more swimmers quitting earlier than any other country, and this large drop-out rate is another competitive situation for which age-group swimming is at least partly responsible. This large 'scrapheap' is of concern to many coaches, but many others point out that the drop-outs still learned to swim better, and got discipline from swimming, while they stayed in it.

This book will endeavour to show how and why age-group works for Americans. It will trace the first age-group champions in this young programme and give some answers you may need in convincing your community you should start such a programme.

3

The Age-Group Founders Talk About Their Brain-Child

AGE-GROUP SWIMMING
by Carl O. Bauer
(Age-Group Chairman 1947–1950.
Father of Age-Group Swimming,
1st National Age-Group Chairman,
and Director of Athletics, Missouri
Athletic Club, St Louis, Mo.)

During the past decade, age-group swimming has become an increasingly interesting and important subject in many committee sessions. Attendance has accordingly increased in the age-group swimming committee meetings of the AAU conventions. The committee chairman, Mrs Beth Kaufman, and now Harold Heller, have conducted proceedings thoroughly and efficiently for many years.

At any given meeting there is the question, a criticism: 'Why doesn't the age-group system extend beyond age 17?' This is a constant query of many people. During the formative years of the age-group programme when our top age-group was 15–16, I was often asked why the graduated scale for competitive swimming did not go into the 17-, 18-, and 19-year-old brackets. My answer is I do not think it sound to reach into national and Olympic competition with age-regulations.

Lately, there have been articles published in national sport and swimming magazines expressing various warnings about the age-group system. Yet the happy fact remains that the activities of the age-group system have become more overwhelming, while the critics are still few.

The thesis of some of the recent warnings is that many youngsters, especially girls, who get a taste of victory, and attain stardom early, too early, too often drop out of swimming prematurely. In answer to this contention, Beth Kaufman, mother of age-group swimming, has taken a stand. As a mother, and as chairman of the AAU age-group swimming committee, she stated, in essence, that orderly and regular competition on the basis of the graduated scale of age-group is just the thing for the youth.

Judging from the facts present, I feel that age-group swimming could well become a controversial item.

An interesting point of view has been taken in Chapter 5 'Where Age-Group May Be Failing Us', by Rose Mary Dawson, a mother, coach, and writer. This truly fine article appeared in *Junior Swimmer-Swimming World* and *Amateur Athlete*. Mrs Dawson speaks of the age-group system in the highest terms, but, as a result of some of her observations, she expresses some doubt and fears. Before proceeding further into her chapter, I would like to point out that the reader of articles dealing with the pros and cons of age-group swimming should be familiar with some of its history in the AAU. Therefore, I would like to digress a bit.

There can be no denial that remodelling the old AAU novice and junior swimming divisions was quite a task. The difficulty lay in overcoming and overruling many outmoded practices. Control of the movement of junior swimmers into national championships and Olympic competition was actually in the hands of a few monopolists and opportunists. A result of this situation was that only a few aquatic stars and champions were developed to their fullest. Many potential stars did not get a chance to gain national recognition, due to the selectivity of the monopolists. The guidance of our nations foremost swimmers and divers was handled by specialty coaches and managers. (A condition was produced which amounted to nearly a fanatical passion, and some of the monopolists are still smouldering over the loss of their powerful positions.) The age-group swimming programme has eliminated those abuses.

The programme got its start in the AAU in 1947 when Lawrence J. Johnson, AAU swimming chairman at that time, was instrumental in getting me elected head of the committee set up to revise the novice and junior swimming competition. The very first meeting, during which the committee was formed, was marked by stormy proceedings and sharp issues. Lauri

27

Johnson supported me for election to the chairmanship and knew I had a definite programme in mind. He knew I had tried and proved years of experience behind me, from the early days in 1915 and 1916 at the Chicago Central Y.M.C.A. to my aquatic work at the Missouri Athletic Club. As swimming chairman of the AAU Ozark Association I had instituted age-group swimming in Ozark and St Louis municipal contests.

During the first three 'evolutionary' years of the age-group swimming programme (from 1948 to 1950), Lauri Johnson never wavered in his support. Of great importance in the task of bringing orderly procedure into novice teenage competition was *not* to take the second step before we had succeeded with the first. The programme was to be simple, appealing, and readily understandable. We hoped for a programme which would be practical and beneficial to all. Upon reviewing this aim in the light of the present-day programme after 15 years of operation, it must be conceded that it is simple, practical, and wholesome.

Those engaged in athletics and progressive youth activities await with keen interest the ultimate development of the age-group system. For while the system is in its second decade, it is still in a state of growth and refinement. Yet because of its universal appeal, the programme is beautiful and fascinating to follow. Activities within age-group swimming are reaching such proportions, it appears that restrictions are now in order.

Mrs Dawson has prescribed a constructive outline by which certain dangers of age-group swimming can be effectively met and handled. Her misgivings about the programme prompted her suggestions aimed at safeguarding the age-group system.

My answer to her qualms revolves around my firm and long-standing conviction that star performers, regardless of age, even though they have proved themselves and have tasted glory, will *not* forego the challenge of their accomplishments nor the responsibilities of their fame. But quite the contrary to quitting, they will not be able to resist the lure of greater achievements yet to be attained. A star performer always seeks perfection in his endeavours, and 'staying in the swim' is part of his demonstration of genuine dedication to the sport. The saying 'Once an athlete, always an athlete' fits quite well here. For while the world may feel that a person who was once an athlete may

28

forget what it means, the true athlete knows within himself he is always an athlete and won't forget it.

Mrs Dawson mentions the situation where five- and six-year-olds are allowed to pursue regularly scheduled competition and are often encouraged in it. Of course this is bad, I agree, and the age-group system was intended to forestall and prevent it. It is unfortunate when a young hero is inclined to quit swimming competition. The truth is that the big-shot youngster is less aware of what he is throwing away when he decides to quit. He does not know that, after improving on a basic ability through competent coaching and training to the point of attaining a high degree of proficiency, it takes comparatively little effort to maintain a winning form and a high standard of performance. It is up to conscientious coaches to let them know what they have at stake, and to keep the would-be quitters in swimming.

Often, when a swimmer is on the way to being a great or even a near-great, he is sorely tempted to give up everything. It is sad to see someone throw away a good thing wilfully through ignorance of what he can yet achieve and what possibilities lie ahead. It is apparent to me, if not to others, that these cases of quitting are not attributable to the age-group system. The other extreme is the problem of swimmers burning themselves out. Here is where the age-group system contributes to the prevention of real trouble.

In conclusion, I would like to urge hopeful athletes and would-be stars, their tutors, parents, officials, and guiding lights, to look into the age-group swimming programme and see wherein its ultimate good lies. Its functions must be safeguarded against abuses, for the system is a good medium for attaining physical excellence and achieving success. I truly believe the age-group system will bring out the best in our people.

AN EVALUATION OF AGE-GROUP SWIMMING
by Beth Kaufman
(AAU National Age-Group
Chairman 1952–1961)

Let's take a moment to go back to 1951, when there was no age-group programme in the United States. Many old timers, if you think back to those days, can tell the young, ambitious parents and coaches what it was like. Remember – there were three classes of competitors. The Novice, a classification allowing a swimmer to compete until he won a 1–2–3 place medal. Then he progressed to the Junior Class, where again he stayed until he won a 1–2–3 place medal. That placed him in the Senior Class. He had arrived . . . he was a senior swimmer.

But it did not always happen that way. If a novice swimmer entered a junior class and won, he was a senior and could never return to the other class. This resulted in raw, untrained 12-year-olds being suddenly moved into the senior bracket, where they were forced to compete against the trained, experienced swimmer. And these senior swimmers, almost unkind, could not and would not teach the manners of swimming to the little 12-year-old who just arrived on the scene. To survive, the youngster needed tremendous desire and fortitude. Recreation department youngsters had no chance. It was the private athletic club that produced the champions.

The Age-Group Programme was formed with the child in mind, and the 10 and under bracket was added. This bracket was to be sort of an introduction to competitive swimming. The distances were short, but still not shorter than those listed in the High School Manual for Girls.

As the age of the child progressed, the distances were increased in all four strokes. But the increase was gradual. The programme has proved itself during the past years as an important part of the overall swimming programme.

Growth creates problems, and growth of the age-group programme has certainly created its share.

Remember, in the past years, coaches worked with either a men's or women's team. Along came Age-Group, with all children training side by side, and then the children grew old and good enough to compete in the Nationals. Now, leading coaches have to train two teams for two usually widely separated National Championships.

A most natural problem is merely the gigantic increase in number of participants. In many areas, no swimming teams of any type existed. Then, after World War II, building boom of new high schools swept America, a pool was considered as a classroom, and thousands of new participants developed from

30

the 'Learn-to-swim' classes at the schools and recreation departments of cities using these pools.

The 6–7–8-year-olds swimming in sanctioned AAU swimming contests has raised a most definite problem to the age-group programme. Has the child of 6 to 8 the knowledge to sign the application for membership for AAU cards? Most 6-year-olds can scarcely write even their names, and as far as knowing the significance of meaning, I feel that it is lost. Is it right to put the pressure on these children? I have been to AAU sanctioned contests and watched it take a 6-year-old 1 minute to swim 25 yards. Is that competition?

It is fun for 6–7–8-year-olds to swim, but is it best for their health and mental growth to be trained like college men? I say NO. If clubs want their sub-age groups to compete, they can form leagues and swim in their own classification.

In the AAU General Rules, and also in the AAU Swimming Handbook, it states that registration for competitors to be 12 years of age, except the Age-Group and Junior Olympic Programmes. These two programmes list registration for the 10 and under. It also states that no athlete can compete in a sanctioned contest unless registered. It is apparent that some rules, age-group or Junior Olympic, are being laughed aside when these 6–7–8-year-old events are held in America. The latest to come to my attention is a Novice Age-Group Championship. I just cannot understand it.

I have been around a long time, and have watched swimmers rise to the top, others retire, some retain their interest and help new swimmers with talks and coaching, and others just disappear. But, in all my years, I have never known any to reach the top when they started at 6–7 years. They retire at about 12.

Our age-group programme was conceived and carefully thought out with the growing child in mind, both for his development as a swimmer, and for his part in the swimming programme. It is known that the 12–17 years are the ages listed to combat juvenile delinquency. Let us not forget the AIMS and PURPOSES of the Programme. Let us think carefully before we go overboard on the 6–7–8-year-olds as competitors.

4

Towards a Better Philosophy in Age-Group Swimming

Because of the popular success of the AAU Age-Group Swimming Programme with its great growth and accomplishment, I think it is time for our coaches, officials, and our mothers, to re-evaluate this programme, looking backward at its strengths and weaknesses, and looking forward to an even more outstanding programme for developing young swimmers. My views are the private views of a girls' club coach, and of a mother of three young age-group swimmers. I shall confine my remarks in this chapter to girls' age-group swimming because the AAU has a unique and exclusive licence in developing women's competitive swimming with little or no help from the YWCA, High Schools and Colleges. For this reason, results in women's swimming, both successes and failures, can be attributed solely to age-group and follow-up senior AAU swim club programmes.

I feel that age-group contests are never an end unto themselves, but a step towards the ultimate goal, which is open competition. We are not, or should not be, concerned with producing 10-year-old or 12-year-old champions, but with teaching fundamentals (strokes, turns, starts, hard work, distance, conditioning, swimming habits) that will take the 10- and 12-year-olds through their swimming apprenticeship, maintaining their interest and happiness so that, at age 13, or 16, or 20, they will have the best chance of making the Olympic team.

OVER EMPHASIS

Age-group swimming in the 10 and under class, and the 11–12 class, provided it is not over emphasized, is a wonderful way to expose girls to competition, and to provide them sustaining interest towards the bigger goal which is open competition, in swimming and in life. In California, for instance, where age-

32

group swimming has attained its greatest success, it is kept on a home association basis, and all age-group contests must be over by six o'clock. Time final contests without the necessity of long preliminaries are becoming more common in many states. In Michigan, we have encouraged hour-long dual contests between the various AAU Swim Clubs. A 10 and under dual contest, we believe, gives the child the feeling of actually swimming for a team and not just working for his own personal glory. The big point of these dual meetings, however, is the matter of time. As a mother, I am very much opposed to keeping young girls at contests lasting from 10 a.m. until 10 p.m. It is hard on them physically to sit all day, or two or three days, around a pool in the emotional strain of a big, long omnibus 300-heat contest. I have seen what a strain this can be to my own daughters. To keep young children at contests all day and on into the night is foreign to our philosophy, and contrary to the best interests of swimming. To let ten- and twelve-year-olds go on swimming trips to distant contests not only keeps them out too late, but jades them to the glamour of travel at a later age when they should be reaching their true potential. There is also the danger of the odd years deflating the swimmer to a point where she feels she was a champion at 10 or 12, and why go back to being a punker at 11 or 13, but this is not necessarily bad training. After all, a high school senior is a big shot who must adjust to being a lowly freshman in college, and so it goes on into life.

15–16–17 AGE-GROUP

There is very little excuse for the 15–16–17 class in girls swimming. A fifteen-year-old girl must be ready to shoot for the open events. The 15–16–17 class is begging the issue. At most contests the 13–14 winners can beat the 15–16–17 winners. 15–16–17 is an important class for boys but it is a lame duck in girls swimming. It is not the object of girls age-group swimming to protect the semi-retired or 'never-was' champions. The senior national champions produced through the age-group programme are ample testimony to the value of this fine programme but an examination of the facts will show that no true champion girl improved a great deal by staying exclusively in the age-group programme after age 13. In areas where age-group swimming is not followed by a good senior programme, the top age-bracket should be 15 and up, rather than 15–16–17. It is not a wholesome attitude when girls dread becoming 18 and feel their competition is then behind them. This is not a healthy situation because the main value of age-group swimming is to get girls through the difficult teens and not abandon them just at the time when they need swimming most.

TOO MANY TROPHIES

Too many age-group contests with too many trophies can spoil a girl for the future and take the kick out of winning 'just another medal' when that medal really means something. Too much publicity, and too much praise from people who do not know swimming, and too many outsized medals and trophies for insignificant performances, can put a premium on mediocrity that the later rewards for really being successful cannot match.

Dr Bogart, a member of the U.S. National Age-Group Committee says 'we are in danger of producing a new breed of humanity known as the two-legged brass-hunters'. Bogart watched a group of St Louis swimmers looking at a magazine cover picture of Don Schollander wearing his four Olympic medals. 'That's nothing,' bragged one boy, 'I won more stuff than that at an age-group contest'.

Joe Louis spoke truly when he said, 'Fat cats don't fight'. To swim fast, you must first swim right. No child should start racing before she has really learned to swim. Racing a child in 25 yds sprints with a bad stroke can ruin her for the distances she will have to swim later. A strong young girl can force her way in a short sprint when she ought to be holding her stroke and developing her stroke for the longer distances in the future.

I believe in age-group competition for youngsters. I believe in starting our girl swimmers young, but all in moderation, and with our ultimate goal the Olympic Games and not the country club championship.

A MEANS TO AN END

I also believe that swimming is not an end in itself but a means to develop strong healthy bodies, grace, and co-ordination, as well as a wonderful way for a girl to learn how to win, and to lose, and to pay the price. Championships are the by-product of training the mind and body to think and act under stress. These are sometimes painful lessons, but less painful when learned in the swimming-pool than when learned much later in the world of adult society. If a child sets swimming goals for herself she should be encouraged, but no pushed or cajoled by an ambitious parent. Swimming-training is good discipline for a child, but it must be fun and never punishment. Swimming can be a marvellous antidote to 'going steady' and to juvenile delinquency.

Although the swimmer must be encouraged when she wins an age-group event, she must also be asked the question 'whom did you beat?' This is important if we believe that our object is to produce Senior and Olympic Champions, with age-group championships merely an important step towards the greater goals in swimming and in life.

This is the philosophy I have resolved where my daughters are concerned, and for the other mothers' daughters on my team. I have thought a great deal about the many goods and the few evils in age-group swimming for girls and I hope my conclusions will help others in promoting this programme, which is the life blood of our swimming future.

5

Where Age-Group May Be Failing Us

As a mother of four, I am proud of my children's accomplishments in age-group swimming. As a mother, I think age-group swimming an entertaining and rewarding way for my children to spend their spare time. It has taught them to swim well, which may some day save their lives. It is a healthy activity, and it keeps them busy. Certainly, as a mother, I see only good in age-group swimming and none of the harm some educators would have us believe comes from exposing our children to competition. This is pure hogwash.

These educators have not viewed children in age-group swimming. I have never known of a child who was harmed by age-group swimming. Hustling my children off to swimming-club practice is at least as valuable as hustling them off to the playground or to day-camp. They are learning to give and take, and to compete as they will have to compete all through life. There are tangible goals to be strived for.

As a mother, I see only good in the programme and I do not spend much time thinking how much more might be done, but as a coach I must take a more long-range view. As a coach, I must protect my sport, so I want to know how age-group fits into our Olympic development programme, how it will keep my girls interested in swimming during their 'troubled teens,' how it fits into our national physical fitness plans, and what effect it will have on senior swimming. I want swimming to provide the necessary rewards to keep swimmers interested, to keep them at it long enough, and old enough for peak physical performance. These are the broad aims I think worthy of our great sport of swimming. As a coach, I want to evaluate age-group against these aims. As my children get older, I will also want these values as a mother. Age-group cannot help me, then, unless it is a carry-through programme.

There can be no doubt that our National AAU age-group

swimming programme under Beth Kaufman has introduced competitive swimming to more people. In ten years, the number of children exposed to the programme annually in America has grown to 500,000 from a starting point of less than 50,000. These are registered athletes only, and the numbers added to include country-club and community-pool programmes not under AAU jurisdiction would be even more staggering. Swimming-pools have become a recognized recreational necessity in all well-planned communities, and each new pool brings with it some kind of swimming programme. Beth Kaufman's committee by its tabulations of times have set standards of excellence for all to view. The stop-watch has made us all honest in our appraisal of our children's progress. The exposure of hundreds of thousands of new swimming enthusiasts, and the establishment of standards, are genuine accomplishments of age-group.

The vast size and rapid growth of the age-group programme have more than justified its existence, but recent developments in the programme have not been encouraging to many serious-minded coaches who formerly endorsed the programme without reservation. In the areas where age-group is biggest, oldest, and strongest, there seems danger of the tail wagging the dog. Age-group has become so dominant that it threatens to take over senior swimming. This danger is particularly noticeable in California where age-group in the past has turned out the greatest number of senior champions. The coaches there, and elsewhere, are alarmed by a downward age trend in competitive swimming interest. In spite of prohibitive legislation at the National AAU Convention, and refusal of the national committee to recognize eight and under records, eight and under events are held at more and more meets. Ambitious promoters out to collect more entry-fees, and ambitious parents out to see their children perform, have subscribed heavily to eight and under, and even six and under, events. The harm in this is not immediately evident, but the results are now able to be determined in areas that have been strong in age-group for a number of years. In some Pacific coast contests, for instance, there are often a dozen heats in the eight and under events with barely enough for a final in the fifteen-sixteen events. In Dayton, Ohio, where they have an exceptionally strong age-group programme

37

for girls, the girls nearly all quit before they reach the fifteen-sixteen age-group. This sort of thing is repeated all over the country, and it is disturbing to many of our most successful coaches.

DALAND ON OVER-EMPHASIS

'I feel very strongly,' says Olympic Coach Peter Daland, 'that we are killing off too many swimmers with over-emphasis in age-group swimming.' Daland expresses distress at great success in years of immaturity, followed by early decline. He conducted a personal survey of his girl swimmers on the 1964 Olympic team, found they were all products of age-group as an exposure programme, but half of them did not have a background of intensive age-group training. Of the remaining half, only a few had early age-group fame as indicated in 10 and Under National Age-Group ratings. These few had been cautiously and cleverly hand-led to retain their interest. 'I do not believe in "pre-natal" contests,' Daland says. 'There is too much proposed legislation aimed at the quick win today, instead of the sound future of our age-group swimmers.'

HAINES ON COMPETITION

'I believe in children learning to swim at five or six,' says Olympic coach George Haines, 'but I don't believe they should go into serious competition and heavy training until they are eleven or twelve.' Haines has been America's most successful coach with young swimmers. His girls become national champions, even Olympic swimmers, at 13, 14, 15, and his boys at 15, 16, 17; yet he feels that starting too early in hard competition is bad.

Until recently, whenever the question was asked, 'To what do you attribute American success at the 1960 and 1964 Olympics?' nearly every authority replied candidly, 'age-group swimming'. Now, these same age-group adherents are beginning to criticize the programme. The age-group girls and boys who made the Olympic team were not the ones who had been exposed to six and under races with all the glory and medals accorded an older champion. The six and under youngsters are just now coming of age, and most of them are dropping out of swimming before they mature enough to try for an Olympic team. When a girl has been acclaimed a National champion at ten, the glory of swimming accomplishment is old stuff to her before she is fifteen. The age-group programme should be a development programme and not an end unto itself, yet ambitious coaches, parents, and local sports editors, like to brag about 'our national champion'. The youngster is blown up so big that he or she cannot take the knocks that must follow before getting big enough, and strong enough, for senior competition. Bragging parents are even worse than the children on this score, preferring to withdraw a child from the programme, or blaming the coach when the child's interest lags because of too many years at it, or because of a fear of being a has-been; then everything good in swimming suffers.

This problem is more serious in newer swimming areas than in the old swim centres that had teams before age-group took hold. In these older areas, senior teams and responsible coaches existed and still do. In fact, it may be these teams and coaches, as much as the age-group programme, that are responsible for the better swimming in the most popular swimming areas. These two factors seem to overlap in Philadelphia, Arizona, California, and Indianapolis, where most of our senior champions develop. Regardless of which came first, the chicken or the egg, the presence of strong senior teams in these areas has kept age-group in perspective. The young swimmers in these areas want to make the big team as much, or more, than they want to set age-group records.

And how do these coaches keep the children interested? The precious ingredient is competition. Competition must be the yard-stick for personal accomplishment and satisfaction in both age-group and senior swimming. Herein lies both the problem and the solution to our problem. Through control of competition we can keep a child interested until he or she matures as a swimmer. We must start out by teaching our child to swim, and five, six, or seven, is the ideal age. Learning how to swim is competition enough for a child this age. A year of play, of getting used to being in and with the water, should follow. Only then do we begin serious swimming-lessons; classwork in new strokes, dives, starts, and turns. When this interest begins to lag, it is time for little races and competition within the class. This can be followed by intra-squad contests. Age-group swimming should be saved as a new thrill to be met in sequence when the swimmer is no longer satisfied with an intramural programme. This is my recommended procedure for very young swimmers if you wish to keep them interested until they are seventeen.

AGE-GROUP MEETS SHOULD BE LOCAL

Once into age-group, the race meeting should be kept local, within the city or the home-association. Wide travel, big trophies, and lots of publicity, should be glamour reserved for the older girls ... the 'varsity. The main reason for these trips is the need for more competition. Only when a swimmer has exhausted the local competition does he or she need to go out of town. Boys and girls starting later can move along the glamour-trail a bit faster, but those starting later are not our problem. Our problem is with the six-, eight-, and ten-year-olds who are already allowed to taste the thrills of big medals and overnight trips. The percentages are against these children continuing their swimming to the age when they can get the most out of it, an age when they will also need it most, and when swimming needs them the most. Studies show that five to seven years is the usual longevity for a competitive swimmer, and in modern high pressure competition it is more often five than seven – particularly with girls. Save these years until your child needs them. Do not waste them in kindergarten swimming.

I repeat, neither as a mother, nor as a coach, am I arguing that age-group swimming harms a six-year-old; I am simply saying that a six-year-old can be kept interested in swimming without participating in an age-group programme, and this is not true later on.

I coach a girls' college team. College girls need physical fitness programmes a lot more than constantly active girls of pre-teen age. I would like to think that a few girls might still have some of their five to seven years' competitive swimming time left to help them through college. Certainly, they should have enough of it left to finish high school. As a mother, I feel my daughters being in a swimming team may keep her from going steady at fourteen, and her fast times in the pool will be a lot safer than fast times in the car.

Just as the relationship between grade school, junior high,

One way other countries can close the gap in age-group swimming is to use their clean lakes and ocean bays and river edges for construction of inexpensive bulkhead pools. This one is at Mrs Dawson's Camp Ak-O-Mak in Canada

Swim champions Suzy Thrasher (U.S.) and Sara Barber (Canada) made the top after extensive age-group training

The late Matt Mann coached children at his daughter's camp. Louise Kennedy (wearing towel) made the 1964 Canadian Olympic team and Elaine Jacques (hands on legs) was in the 1959 Pan-American Games

high school, and college sports, is a well defined progression known and understood by the general public, so the AAU progression from swimming classes to age-group, to senior competition, must be weighed to keep our records honest, and to keep our children swimming. Until this is done, age-group, while a fine thing in itself, will not be doing the whole job it can do to promote better swimming.

As long as high school, and junior high school principals and athletic departments refuse to recognize the need for a 'varsity type athletic programme for girls, we must provide it through the AAU, and age-group must help promote this.

6

The Structure of Age-Group Swimming

So what is Age-Group? In the United States, it is 500,000 swimmers competing in age classification 10 and under, 11–12, 13–14, 15–16–17. There are 690 events accepted for national age-group records, events swum in 20 yd pools, 25 yd pools, 25 mtr pools; in 50 yd pools, 55 yd pools and 50 mtr pools. National ratings of the five best times in each event, each age-group, and each length pool, are compiled each year.

Structurally, Age-Group Swimming is organized as follows:
NATIONAL AAU
Men's Swimming Committee
Women's Swimming Committee
Sub-committees:
Sub-committees:
Age-Group Swimming
Men's Diving
Women's Diving
Water Polo
Long Distance Swimming
Women's Water Polo
This national organization is duplicated on a state or association level. The men's and women's committees meet separately, and jointly, on many matters as to rules, diving, water polo, and particularly age-group swimming.

The National AAU is a federation deriving its authority from 53 local associations, often, but not always, organized along state lines, hence there is a Michigan Association but a Middle Atlantic Association of several states, and there are three associations, Metropolitan, Adirondack, and Niagara Frontier, in New York State. Each association has voting representation in the parent AAU, and in the various committees, plus a duplicate of the above organization pattern on a local level.

In America the National Age-Group Chairman, and his committee composed of a representative elected by and from each of 44 local Associations, (only 44 of the 53 have age-group programmes) recommend action to the parent men's and women's swimming committees. The age-group sub-committee has the power to administrate its sport by approving, or disapproving, new records, etc. The sub-committees biggest job is compiling annually the five best times in each of 690 events from best times certified by the 44 regional chairman, or their records sub-chairman. Within the local (regional) Associations, ground-rules can be written, but National suggests, and accepts, records and times only in accordance with national rules. Hence an association may hold 8 and under races but not with the approval of the National body which will not accept such a classification. On the other end of the scale, National, and most Associations, accept 15 to 17 records, but some Associations have thrown out this class as begging the issue. In these areas, the classification is sometimes called '15 and up', and sometimes 'open', depending on whether the area is primarily age-group oriented, or senior-swimming oriented. The former 15–16 classification was changed to 15–17 a few years ago as a compromise to include most secondary school children who might be cut out after 16 in an area that had a good age-group programme but a weak senior programme. The battle had been between those who wanted to protect the 16-year-olds from college-age competitors, and those who wanted more open events in age-group meets and wanted the 15–16 division thrown into the open classification, which is what has been done in Canada instead of adding 17.

The difficulty in any device different from the national classification was that a 15-year-old could not set an age-group record in a 15 and over, or open event. This was changed in 1963 after four years of bitter debate between elements wishing to protect the development programme feeling it would discourage swimming to open it and *vice versa*.

There is great division of opinion on 8 and under, and on 15 and over – on the amount of travel, the size of medals and trophies, and the length of age-group meets. These things are being reviewed and legislated constantly, on both local and national levels. There is universal acceptance, however, of the age-group principle at 10 and under, 11–12, 13–14 age-groups.

43

This is the exposure to competition period, the growing period where a child needs to try his luck against his own age and strength. There is some argument favouring an older period, 15–17 for boys, but not for girls who mature earlier. There is mixed opinion among top-coaches as to when a child should begin hard training, and what kind of training. Some areas hold out for short events in the early ages, and others, notably Florida, argue that strength, and proper mental attitude, are built by longer events early, building up the body, and the technique for the short speed events later.

Many coaches, and parents, would just as soon have a 10-year-old champion as an open champion, and these exponents want hard training early. A mother may not be interested in her daughter swimming at 14 or 17, and so is not concerned about long-range benefits, or defects from early exposure and/or hard training at 9 or 10. In the United States, where senior swimming still controls age-group within the AAU at the national level, there is an effort to temper this frank local interest in pre-teen swimming with the national and international efforts of the U.S. to develop competitive teams at an open level. Many top-coaches want technique engrained in each youngster before he tries to swim fast. Others may feel the competition must come soon, and fast, to hold the child's interest (more on this in other chapters).

Many of the regional Associations once had rules against registering and issuing cards to competitors under 12 years of age. Age-Group has obviously changed all this, raising many questions in debate as to at what age a child can be held responsible as a signee of the amateur code, etc. The Association Registration Chairman is not always a swimming man, and it is sometimes quite difficult to explain to a former boxer why an athlete needs to be registered at 8. The regional associations control the conduct of age-group swimming contests at local sponsors level by the issuing of sanctions which can be withheld if the local sponsor insists, for example, on having 6 and under, or 8 and under, competition, if these classifications have been ruled contrary to the best interests of the local AAU, of local swimming, or of amateur sports in that area.

The 690 Age-Group events contested in age-group swimming break down into 345 events for boys, and 345 events for girls.

Records and best five times each year are compiled in six different length swimming-pools – 20 yds, 25 yds, 25 mtrs, 50 yds, 50 mtrs, and 55 yds. The 20 yd pools are common in older YMCA pool areas. (See Appendix I for complete list.) 25 yd and 25 mtr pools are called *short course* while the 50 yd, 55 yd, and 50 mtr pools are called *long course*. The vast U.S. indoor programme; age-group, school, and college, is contested primarily in 25 yd pools.

The outdoor (summer) season is long course, where the longer pools are available, but there is nothing to prevent record applications, summer or winter, in any or all of the six length pools acceptable to the age-group committee.

20 YD POOL EVENTS ARE:
  40 yd sprints in all *four* strokes.
  100 yds in *all* strokes.
  80 and 160 yds Individual Medley.
  160 yds Medley and Freestyle Relays at *10 and under*.
These events jump to 50, 100, and 200, in the *25 yd and 25 mtr pools;* to 50, 55, 100, and 110, in *50 yd, 50 mtr, and 55 yd pools.*
  11–12 age division include all 10 and under events, plus 200 freestyle and 400 relays.
  13–14 age divisions – add 200s in each stroke.
  15–16–17 age divisions – add 400 Individual Medley and 400 Freestyle in each length pool.
These age-group events, like all swimming, produce an amazing number of broken records each year. The 1964 results were as follows:

Total number of events reported : 676.

GIRLS :   339
BOYS :   337

GIRLS

Age			No. Events	Records Broken or Tied	%
10–under	...	...	69	34	50
11–12	...	...	84	52	62
13–14	...	...	90	60	67
15–17	...	...	96	79	82

45

BOYS

10–under	...	...	68	34	50
11–12	...	...	84	50	60
13–14	...	...	90	53	59
15–17	...	...	95	69	74

NOTE: The smallest percentage of records broken was in the 10 and under class, indicating that coaches are spending more time now, teaching the youngest children how to swim, and less time training the young swimmers to break records. This is a healthy trend. Records will be broken as natural talent comes to the fore, but developing this talent technique-wise will show better results later on in record-breaking. It is gratifying that the percentage of records broken graduates in direct proportion to the age of the swimmers. This lends statistical weight to the conclusion that age-group 1964 definitely kept its perspective, and its progression, towards better senior swimming. It indicates hopefully that age-group swimming has come of age.

With events established at both national and local levels, Association Swimming Committees will usually meet with various sub-committees to arrive at time standards and schedules which will regulate the number of contests, the type of contests (A or B), time final or preliminary and final; when, where, how long, how late, and how often. Each club sponsoring contests is a member of the Association and so has a voice in deciding Association policy just as the Association representatives to the National Convention have a voice and a vote in establishing national policy.

The Joint National Men's and Women's Swimming Committee of the AAU operates as an organ of F.I.N.A. The AAU is an umbrella organization holding U.S. jurisdiction for twelve International Sports Federations. There are both advantages and disadvantages to such an arrangement.

7

Organizing an Age-Group Swim Club

The day is past when a lot of money was needed to start a swimming club. Any group of parents can start a club by renting pool time, and hiring a coach. Getting a charter from the AAU, or any national swimming federation, is for the asking. The club can operate on a pay-as-you-go basis.

The secret of running a good age-group swimming club is essentially the same as running any sports group. The sport must be fun for the competitors, and the coach must get some satisfaction out of the work. The coach must have authority, almost absolute authority, and he must have a very close relationship with his swimmers. The younger the swimmers, the more they must adore the coach. There must be organization, and communication, with parents since many of the children are very young, but parent interference has wrecked, and will wreck, most swimming clubs. Get a strong-willed coach, and let him be a dictator in the pool, a pleasant dictator we hope, but a dictator nevertheless. Some coaches allow no parents in the pool during practice, and others allow them in the grandstand but not on the pool deck. In either case, it is advisable for a parent not to interfere. As a buffer against over-zealous parents, there should be a swimming manager, or swimming club chairman, who works for, and with, the coach on administrative matters. Most clubs have a parent council, or board of directors. The coach should be a member of this executive, and any complaints on his conduct of affairs as a coach, or as an administrator, should be voiced at the monthly meeting of the executive, or at the annual meeting.

The coach-parent relationship is not all one way. The parents must have recourse if the coach is over-zealous, or under-zealous, but these things should be worked out, and talked out, in the meetings, and not hashed over at home, or at the pool, or on the phone, with other mothers. There should be some machinery whereby parents, and coach, can communicate in establishing the best way that they can help their child's swimming, and the best way their child can get the best the swimming club has to offer with the least possible disruption of home life. This relationship is sometimes like walking a tightrope, for both parent and coach. Balance is difficult.

Some coaches rely heavily on parent committees to raise money, arrange transportation, publicity, entry blanks, health certificates, etc., and others prefer to do most of the work themselves rather than to co-ordinate and administrate the complexities of a volunteer parent-organization. Here again, a manager or chairman who knows the coach, can be of great assistance.

Most clubs require parent help in officiating at meets, and driving to contests. It takes a great many people, and it is common for parents who do the work to complain about parents who do not do the work. This is human nature, but it is also a dangerous situation. Many an age-group swimmer has dropped out because his, or her, parents did not want to get up and drive to early morning practice, or spend their weekends officiating at swimming-contests. The parent made to feel guilty after turning down persistent phone-calls asking him to perform these duties, will often find an excuse to pull his child out of the club. Most coaches would prefer to honour in some way the parents who do the work, rather than lose the children of parents who do not choose to serve.

Many parents enjoy going to the contests, and these people are happier if they do have a job that contributes to the success of their child's swimming programme.

The delicate relationship between an age-group coach, his children, and his parents, is unique in age-group swimming. It is a much more difficult balance to maintain than confronts the high school or college coach with institutional backing. It can be most rewarding, but there is not a coach alive who has not said, 'deliver me from parents,' at least once. There is no way to have age-group swimming without parents. I take this matter up in Chapter 11 – 'The Age-Group Parent, Jekyll or Hyde?'

8

Age-Group Training. Is it Different?

You need a pool, a coach, and some rules, to keep order. Other than this, I prefer to believe there is no such thing as age-group training being different from any other training. I believe in the carrot-in-front-of-the-donkey type of incentive programme, no matter what the age, but especially in age-group. This calls for competition rationed to keep interest high. The first challenge is, learning to swim, Learn-to-swim classes provide the challenge of conquering the fear of the water, and then mastering techniques of conquest of the water itself. This progression feeds on the competitive nature of children. They have a desire to win, and to beat each other, to improve their techniques, while doing so is a matter of praise and correction in some delicate blend. Age-group contests should begin when intra-squad racing is no longer adequate competition to keep a child interested. The tragedy is to teach a child to race before he learns to swim well and correctly. Short age-group races can encourage this racing with brute strength and no technique. Age-group races should measure, and inspire, children to work harder on technique, and not to thrash the water. It is a difficult balance to keep. In some areas, and in some competitions within any given area, the races should be kept short so that as many swimmers as possible can participate in a short meet, so that coaches can screen talent in greater numbers, and earmark potential for further schooling. In other areas, and in other spots within the same area, age-group races should be long, to establish work and conditioning patterns, to build strength, and to force efficient swimming; to see that those who swim well finish well, that those who do not swim well will not splash and slash their way to deceiving wins that will betray them later in longer races for older swimmers. Perhaps, at different times, during the same season, a coach can offer the mile races and the 5o's.

49

The Konrads were trained as young children to swim miles. Hendricks swam distance as a youngster, sprinted to an Olympic title later after the distance swimming plus his size, age, and weight, training had made him strong enough to sprint fast.

We call it the YMCA triangle. It is not the way they swim in most YMCA's, but it makes sense. An upside down triangle with the distance work, the long line on top sharpening with conditioning, and strength, and time, to a very sharp point late in each season, and late in the career to speed.

This may be hard to sell, but the little boy or girl who likes to swim distance, who develops rhythm and stroke efficiency, strength, endurance, a sense of pace, and CONFIDENCE, in his or her ability to swim *far*, and then *far and fast*, can later swim fast, then faster, and build down to a fast 200 or 100 so much easier than the early 50 man trying later for the condition, the habit, and the confidence, to build up to hundreds and two hundreds.

Most successful age-group coaches say that age-group coaching is no different from senior swimming so far as types of work-out are concerned. I believe it depends on the starting point, the skill level and the attitudes to be dealt with. Generally, I do not ask my swimmers for school year two-a-day work-outs, until I think these are necessary. This may be at age 11, 12, 13, or never. Kathy Ellis and Cynthia Goyette, to name two Olympic gold medal winners, simply do not thrive on two-a-day 'rock 'em, sock 'em' California work-outs, but most modern swim champions do thrive on two a day, on hard work, and more hard work.

The most successful 10 and under, age-group swimmers are those that train, and work, the hardest, but there is considerable doubt in my mind as to the desirability of training a 10 and under champion. George Haines, who has the greatest number of 14–15–16-year-old champion-all-class swimmers, says he doesn't believe in starting hard interval work-outs until 11 or 12, whatever the best age to start something, they hope to finish at the Olympic games.

This is not to say hard training will stunt growth, or harm a child physically. It will not, but, psychologically, it is best to wait until 11 or 12 to start hard training.

So the work-outs for 6 to 10 age swimmers, or 6 to 8 and

9 to 11, or some such combination, terminating at 12 for girls, and 13 for boys, can be light and busy with stroke. It can be long and busy with counting up the miles, with games, and stunts and exercises, form swimming and fun races. Age-group in these early years is to keep it interesting. Age-group has produced no Olympic girl champions younger than 14, no boys younger than 17, and these ages are the top level of effective age-group swimming for a girl (14) and boy (17). Although, in rare cases, a girl or boy may mature later, a mass exposure programme like age-group races must be designed for the majority with the coach deciding when and where he wants to use age-group to stimulate his individual boys and girls, his team as a whole.

Ten and under races should be taken in stride. This is why most people on the U.S. age-group committee favour keeping these races short. But they must also encourage good stroking, and this is why 50's and 100's have replaced 25's. Age-groupers are imitators, and so they will want interval training, work-outs, special diets, when to go to bed rules, etc. Summer work-outs can be tougher than winter, and two-a-day, but, again, the big problem is sustaining interest for the high pressure over the years when the children are old enough, and strong enough, to make a run for the top. This means novelty at 10, leading up to ritual at 12, and habit at 14.

An age-group work-out in stressing technique can add variety with starts, and turns, and push-offs. No Olympic winner had a poor start, or missed a turn. This took hours and hours at the end of a pool, busy work to fill the longer rest intervals, cross-pool work when the pool is crowded, fun and challenge to young age-groupers perfecting a tumble turn, learning how to blast off on a start, timing in and out off the wall from 10 yards out so that a swimmer can learn how much easier it is to take off time on the ends rather than the centre of the pool, the art of pace, and the feel of rhythm, the number of strokes and the number of breaths, and when and how to breathe. All these things, and more, with the early races, quizzes but not a final exam.

What an age-group work-out should contain is elementary. Any good coaching-book lists work-outs. They all have some distance, sprints, interval, locomotive, or endless relay. Kicking

51

and/or pulling and/or whole stroke, specializing in one stroke, or training with all four. It is as Mark Twain described people. All pretty much the same, but it is the difference that makes them interesting. Children must have fun, and being on a team is fun, but they must also have pride in accomplishment, and that comes from individual achievement. The age-group coach must know his trade – he is a teacher first and a trainer second, as opposed to the senior coach who is first a trainer. Early age-group races must not make the training more important than the teaching, and late age-group races are worthless unless they show that the teaching will not pay off any longer without hard training.

Trainer-teacher, or Teacher-trainer, whichever it is, an age-group coach is first, last, and always, a psychologist. If he is not, then alert youngsters will not stay with anything as dull as endless laps and sore eyes. The very boredom of the conditions required to become a successful swimming champion challenge the mental concentration of a swimmer far more than his physical limitations.

9
Age-Group Diving

Age-group diving is of necessity different from age-group swimming in several ways, but the basic idea of boys and girls competing in organized competitions with other children of their same ages has worked in stimulating diving as it has in swimming. Divers seem to mature more slowly than swimmers, and they stay with it much longer, so the 15–16–17 age division in diving is much more important than in swimming, where a 15-year-old is usually ready to take his place in senior or open events. There may also be a reason to retain the old novice classifications within age-groups in lieu of time standards for A and B meets in diving.

Age-group diving is not as widespread as age-group swimming, and it is just beginning to take hold, but progress is none the less rapid in the United States where 24 AAU Associations posted a full range of 1963 age-group champions with still more in 1964. Many other Associations, my own in Michigan, for example, held a series of age-group diving contests but did not submit champions for posting with the national tabulations. The Michigan contests begin with just one dive, front dive, in the first contest, and each diver does this dive three times. The second contest adds a back dive, etc. – three back dives, and a repeat on the front dive. This keeps up until all five required dives have been stressed. Whether your programme needs to begin with such elementary diving, or whether you can demand a full list, is a matter of the diving level in your area. Perhaps the answer is this Michigan beginner programme as a novice build-up to the quality you want in your age-group championships.

We have asked Nick Rodionoff, the Southern Pacific (California) AAU Age-Group Diving Chairman and diving coach of the San Fernando Valley Athletic Club to write this chapter on age-group diving – 'What It Has Done For Us And Can Do For You'.

AGE-GROUP DIVING by Nick Rodionoff

A few years ago our S.P.A.A.A.U. area was considered the centre of the top flight senior divers with such National and Olympic Champions as Pat McCormick, Gary Tobian, Dick Conners, Willie Ferrell, Juno Irwin Stover, Paula Jean Meyers, Bob Webster, and Sammy Lee. As these senior divers stepped out of the competitive picture, we found that our area was suddenly lacking in outstanding senior divers. A rebuilding programme was necessary, and our area turned to age-group diving to develop our new champions. Our programme was met with immediate response, in fact our major problem was the large amounts of entries in our age-group diving contests.

A new National Rule was adopted, requiring all age-group divers to do all five basic dives plus at least one optional for ten years or older, and requiring age-groupers, thirteen years or older, to do a full Olympic list (five required, and five optional). This meant that even the very young divers would have to learn the reverse dive, although the rules stated that a diver could omit a dive, and take zeros on that dive. The repercussions of this rule change left us with only a few age-group divers that would still participate in our A.A.U. meets.

NEW COACHING TECHNIQUES

After the uproar from parents and coaches subsided, our area started to develop our age-group divers into divers that could do the new required list of dives. New techniques were necessary, new safety precautions were evolved, and within another year our programme was again producing a good number of divers. Within another year, our programme was as big as ever, with the 1963 California State Age-Group diving Championships having 96 divers entered in four different age-groups.

DIVING QUALITY IMPROVES

The most significant part of this rule change was that the quality of age-group diving improved. We found that our age-group divers were now capable of competing in senior contests. During the next season, our senior diving was completely dominated by age-group divers, who were also able to do well in the National Championships. Linda Cooper (19), Susie Gossick(16), Patty Simm (15), and Shirley Teeples (15), were all

54

able to make the finals in either the Indoor or Outdoor Women's National Championships. Susie Gossick dives for the Westlake Athletic Club, and is coached by Lyle Draves. Patty Simms, Linda Cooper, and Shirley Teeples dive for the City of Commerce, and are coached by Jack Roth. Alan Kara (17), who represents the San Fernando Valley Athletic Club, finished ninth, just .04 of a point away from the finals in the Senior Men's Outdoor National Championships. Larry Andreason (17), who represents the City of Commerce, did little or no age-group diving in 1962. In 1963, Larry, under the direction of Jack Roth, competed in a full age-group and senior diving schedule, all of which helped him to gain consistency. Larry won the Men's Senior National three mtr crown, won the Jr National Tower Championship, and was placed second in the Senior National Tower Championship, in 1963 season's Outdoor Nationals. Larry also represented the U.S.A. in the team that competed in Japan (1963) and won an Olympic bronze medal in 1964.

DIVING CHANGES

Of course, any experienced diving-coach will tell you that fundamentals are vital in diving, and that a diver should not go into the more difficult dives too soon. This, of course, is true, but one must remember that diving has changed tremendously in the last couple of years. Dives that were very rarely seen in competition, are now standard dives. The Forward $3\frac{1}{2}$ somersault was considered a poor risk. Now, at a degree of difficulty of 2.9, and with many divers being able to receive a judge's score of six or higher on this dive, it is almost a pre-requisite for a diver who hopes to be placed in the top six in the Senior Men's National Championships. Reverse $2\frac{1}{2}$, Inward $2\frac{1}{2}$, Backward $2\frac{1}{2}$, $2\frac{1}{2}$ twisting Back $1\frac{1}{2}$, $2\frac{1}{2}$ twisting Reverse $1\frac{1}{2}$, and even triple twisting front $1\frac{1}{2}$, are all becoming quite common dives in top flight Senior Men's Diving. We find that these dives are beginning to show up in Women's Diving as well, with such dives as Double twisting Forward $1\frac{1}{2}$, $1\frac{1}{2}$ twisting Reverse $1\frac{1}{2}$ som., and $1\frac{1}{2}$ twisting Back $1\frac{1}{2}$ som. are becoming common. This next season will see some of our top women divers doing Inward $2\frac{1}{2}$, Back $2\frac{1}{2}$, Reverse $2\frac{1}{2}$ som. and Forward $3\frac{1}{2}$ som. Of course, degree of difficulty does not mean much if the

55

diver can not score well on the dive. The point is, that our present senior divers are becoming capable of scoring as well on a 2.9 dive as any other diver can score on a 2.2 dive. When a diver can score 60 or 70 points on one dive, the importance of learning this type of dive can not be overlooked. Degree of difficulty has also become a factor in choosing the position of the basic dives. The front dive layout at 1.6, if done equally well, can easily out-score the front dive pike at 1.3. Without going into a complete discussion of degree of difficulty, constistency, and ease of execution, of various dives, it is sufficient to say that the present day diver, working towards the National Championships, should develop a list of dives that he or she will be able to score (for 11 dives) around 425 points for women, and 475 points or more for men.

AGE-GROUP DIVING CHANGES

As the times continue to get faster in senior swimming, new techniques are evolving in age-group swimming. Weight training, isometrics, principles of kinesiology, concentrics, interval training, speed play, new stroke techniques, etc. are all being used by coaches attempting to meet the challenge of ever faster times. Diving-coaches as well must 'keep up with the times'. The hurdle and press take on new importance with the stress on lift necessary to do the more difficult dives. The proper arm action is becoming very necessary to do the more difficult dives. The proper arm action is becoming so necessary that many divers are weight-training to develop more power in the adductors. Basic mechanics and fundamentals must be taught. Twisting mechanics must be correct from 'the ground up'. If a young diver is allowed to 'hip twist' (starting the twist before the somersault by twisting the hips away from the centre line of the body) into a full twisting forward somersault, the chances of this diver ever doing a proper double or triple twisting $1\frac{1}{2}$ are almost non-existent. Somersault techniques have also changed and must be presented to the young diver in order for him to execute the multiple somersaulting dives.

A FEW EXAMPLES

In the recent California State Age-Group Diving Championships, age-group divers showed that they were rapidly meeting

Suzy Thrasher, U.S. National Water Polo Champion and National
Collegiate and National Junior Swimming Champion was one of
Mrs Dawson's best age-group protéges

Marty Sinn, world's (15 and 25 mile) marathon record-holder, grew up in Rose Mary Dawson's age-group programme and still trains with the children. One secret of age-group success is group dynamics, when the older swimmers help the youngsters and become coaches

the challenge of this 'new' diving. Ten-year-old Bonnie Adair of the San Fernando Valley Athletic Club concluded an undefeated season by scoring 6, or higher, on all basic dives, and $6\frac{1}{2}$ on a double som. pike. Mike Sullivan, from the San Francisco area, won the boys 11 and 12, using a Forward $2\frac{1}{2}$ som. pike, $1\frac{1}{2}$ twisting back $1\frac{1}{2}$, and an Inward $1\frac{1}{2}$ som. pike, scoring 6 or 7 on all eight of his dives. Thirteen-year-old Jerrie Adair of the S.F.V.A.C. won her second straight State title, scoring 6's and 7's on all 10 of her dives, including a For. $2\frac{1}{2}$ som. pike, Back $1\frac{1}{2}$ som. layout, Inward $1\frac{1}{2}$ som. pike, full twisting Forward $1\frac{1}{2}$ som., and Reverse $1\frac{1}{2}$ som. Fourteen-year-old Don McAlister of Madera used a Forward $3\frac{1}{2}$ som., Inward $2\frac{1}{2}$ som., and Double twisting Forward $1\frac{1}{2}$ som., scoring well on all of his dives. In the 15–17 age group, Patty Simms from City of Commerce won with a high degree of difficulty, and a consistently good performance. Sue Gossick of Westlake A.C. was second, and Shirley Teeples of City of Commerce (going for a tough list, including a Reverse $2\frac{1}{2}$, and Back $2\frac{1}{2}$, and Inward $2\frac{1}{2}$) missed one dive, and finished third. In the boys 15–17, Larry Andreason was on tour in Japan, leaving the Championships up to Alan Kara and Rusty McCarthy of the San Fernando Valley A.C. Both boys used Reverse $2\frac{1}{2}$, and Back $2\frac{1}{2}$, but Kara using a Forward $3\frac{1}{2}$, and Reverse $2\frac{1}{2}$ twisting $1\frac{1}{2}$ won the title.

PLAN YOUR OWN AGE-GROUP PROGRAMME

In conclusion, it can be stated that there is a definite correlation between a good age-group diving programme and a resulting accomplished senior diving programme. If you want a progressive age group programme you will have to plan it around the capability of the divers in your district. Some districts should use a programme of only 1 mtr diving with a limited list (four or five) of dives, districts with more accomplished divers should develop a programme that is in line with the level of achievement of their divers (the S.P.A.A.A.U. District allows all age-groups, including 10 and under, to use the three mtrs board, plus an age-group tower diving programme). Your programme should stress the importance of a continuity of progressions. Many coaches will keep a younger diver from advancing in accordance with his ability, and then, quite suddenly, require the diver to work at maximum effort for prolonged periods. The physical and mental effects of this type of training can be not only demoralizing but hazardous. It is important to the coach to adjust to the progress of each diver, so that performance is commensurate with his ability. Set up a workable programme and work towards a goal.

10

Junior Olympics and Other Age Plans

In Chapter 2 we discussed the possibility of grade-groups organized through the school as an alternative to age-group swimming. There are other plans patterned on age-group, and all such plans in the U.S.A., including age-group, owe their original inspiration to Little League Baseball, the first nationally organized youth sport programme outside the Y.M.C.A. Little League was organized to overcome a trend in which 'the national sport' hardball (hard baseball) was losing to softball, football, basketball, and other activities, both in grade-schools and on the 'sand lots' where boys' interest in sport begins. Little League is local, state, national, and international. It started in Williamsport, Pennsylvania, and the annual world championship is played there at the end of each summer. The first Little Leaguer to reach the Major Leagues was Joey Jay of the Cincinnati Reds.

This Little League exposure programme, like age-group swimming, started children off in the sport. It helped overcome the fear of hard baseball, and reversed the trend away from baseball in the interests of children. It educated fearful parents, introduced safeguards, regulated playing conditions, age classifications, officiating, and obtained sponsors to buy uniforms, equipment, and to take care of travel expenses. Little League, just as AAU, is a regulatory organization, and all financial obligations and local management are left to private sponsors. Little League has three other problems in common with Age-Group Swimming – over zealous parents who would 'kill the umpire', local recreation administrations who dislike the national, state, and district travel, so set up their own rival baseball programmes, and the lack of follow-through from Little League interest to senior baseball. Babe Ruth League Ball and American Legion Ball have been designed to fill age gaps after the would-be ball players graduate from Little League.

59

American football has also adopted the Little League plan.

In the Olympic sports of swimming, diving, track and field (athletics), gymnastics, wrestling, judo, and basketball (proposed), the A.A.U. has organized a Junior Olympic programme. This programme was started after age-group swimming was already well established, and most swimming people feel that Junior Olympics, while fine in other sports, are too much a duplication in swimming. Two such programmes in one sport are unnecessary, and too many versions of the premature champion are not to the best interest of the sport.

In a country, or an area just beginning an age-regulated youth development programme, however, there is a choice. Junior Olympics could be better than Age-Group in such a new area, or maybe a combination of the two. John B. Kelly, Jr and Howard Bissell, Jr have been the first two national chairman of the Junior Olympic programme, and Ken Pettigrew, the swimming chairman. Their programme is advertised as 'a proven plan promoting the American traditions of fair play, good sportsmanship, and clean competition'. Sportsman Kelly, in his early administration of the programme, tried very hard not to overlap the age-group programme in which his wife, Mary, is one of the leading U.S. swim coaches at the Philadelphia Vesper Boat Club.

Basically, Junior Olympics is a seasonal sport, and age-group is a year-round sport. Junior Olympics are limited to one final contest in each state with neighbourhood, metropolitan, sectional, and district, finals leading up to this championship, if necessary. Only the winners and finalists in these state championships are eligible for the annual national ratings of five best times, and for junior Olympic records. Junior Olympic contest times cannot be used in applying for national, or local, age-group ratings, and vice-versa. The Junior Olympic plan, like Operation Mexico described in Chapter 14, presents a champion under contest conditions on a given championship day, much like the Olympics or a national championship, whereas an age-group champion, or record-holder, can swim the time in any legitimate contest. We can argue back and forth for hours over which is the more true indication of sport prowess.

Junior Olympics in swimming are limited to one championship contest in a 25 yd pool and one championship in a 50 mtr pool which eliminates the multi-pool-length claims to national records which reach astronomical numbers in age-group, producing an occasional unexpected champion because the 400 yd individual medley may be contested only once or twice a year in a 50 yd pool in some obscure area with very poor swimming. The Junior Olympic programme has tried very hard to be different from the age-group programme and, in many ways, I believe it is a better programme but it did come later, and participation is not so universal. It is, therefore, a duplication and, in some ways, an abuse, in that the Junior Olympic times are nearly always inferior to age-group times and records in the same standard length pool events. The use of the term 'Junior Olympic' is by permission of the National Olympic Organization, but this label is controversial among knowledgeable swimming enthusiasts who feel it takes the Olympic name too lightly. It is popular with the public, however, and it catches on with the press much better than the labels on age-group programmes.

In any event, Age-Group or Junior Olympic programmes must vary to suit each sport and country. Track age-groups and seasons are slightly different than swimming age-groups and seasons.

In a predominately school and team sport such as basketball, where the sport usually begins in high school at about age 14, a Junior Olympic club programme has been proposed for 11–12–13 only. One age-group limited to children from the 7th and 8th grades in school. This programme is proposed as an exposure and development programme to set up rules and standards leading up to school basketball which is essentially 14 and over. Since this is a new programme, there is a choice. School districts already using competition between Junior High Schools (7th, 8th, 9th grades) will probably not need such a programme and school districts which do not have Junior High basketball will now have a choice of starting a school programme or deferring their young athletes to outside clubs. In any event, I believe high school is too late to start competitive exposure programmes in any sport if we are to lead up to Olympic excellence, or senior competition on a high level. The schools can do the job better than we can if they will do it. If they will not, then children and parents have a recourse through Age-

Group, through Junior Olympics, and through a third over-lapping programme, the AAU Olympic Development Satellite plan which provides each Olympic sport with funds to develop its own youth programmes. That these programmes overlap is unfortunate. Everybody wants to get into the act and this enthusiasm is certainly better with three programmes competing than with no programme for competition. All programmes follow the psychology and philosophy of age regulation as first introduced by Carl Bauer in Age-Group Swimming.

11

The Age-Group Parent—Jekyll or Hyde?

I am one of many swimming coaches who has complained that the main thing wrong with age-group swimming is the age-group parent. I do not know if the men coaches will agree, but I am going to take a woman's most widely used prerogative and change my mind. Evidence has been piling up that the complex two-headed, black-moustached character known as 'the typical Age-Group parent' is not at all typical.

I have had a chance to study this under ideal conditions. At my summer camp, catering almost exclusively to age-group swimmers, we have the youngsters without their parents. I find in 3 out of 4 cases that a child will swim better, and work harder, because he or she responds favourably to the parent's urging. In less than one out of four cases do I see or sense rebellion. Most children want to please their parents, and many of them will work harder for a mother, or a father, than for anyone else.

This does not mean I approve of parent-coaches, but I am beginning to think I do approve of parent-trainers working in co-operation with professional coaches. I believe the much-ridiculed 'over zealous' sports parent needs a defence counsel. It only happens in sports. We would not have a single concert pianist if we did not make thousands of children take their piano lessons. Certainly no one criticizes making a child with talent practise the piano. Even with children who are tone-deaf we do not criticize their parents as much as we do an age-group mother who makes even the most talented swimmer practise. I agree that a swimmer has to want to swim, and that a pianist has to want to play the piano, but never as much as they need to practise to achieve the success they dream of. Very young children often have to be told what they want – this is an age-group parent's job, as distasteful as it might be to many of us. We do not call a child a pianist unless that child plays well, and we should not call every child who swims a swimmer, but if we are going to have either a child pianist, or a child swimmer, there must be hard work, and this means the added incentive, authority, and discipline, of a parent who demands hours of practice.

The parent who finds his child has a talent must push it. 'The good all-round child' is as much a myth as 'the typical age-group parent'. We are inclined to produce a school culture where every child tries everything and never has to pay the price of real accomplishment in anything. By letting a child jump to something new everytime the old gets a bit tedious, we are doing that child a great disservice. Motivation is a complicated mechanism. Children must usually think it is fun, but not always, and they will learn to hate us if we let them quit the first time they lose interest.

Study the teenagers in your own community, as I have in Ann Arbor. Those with an unconditioned commitment to swimming, to music, to excellence in anything, must organize their time, and must go to practise at a regular time, regardless of their current whim. This sort of discipline is the most important single lesson that comes from dedication to a sport. It is also the important factor most lacking in our culture, and most necessary to success in our culture. It cannot begin within the child without a firm push by the parents. The world is full of people unhappy in their work, yet we deplore 'the poor child' who is forced to develop some special God-given talent.

The boys and girls with an unconditional commitment to swimming will invariably do better in everything else they undertake. We have proved this by plotting the grade curve of our best swimmers in and out of season, and against the not so dedicated swimmers, and the non-swimmers. In season, the grades are better, and in or out of season the well-disciplined sports competitors are better. Swimming demands this sort of discipline. More than any other activity available to children, it is a conditioning sport requiring constant training. Even a 100-metre swimming race is an endurance event requiring more than raw talent. Children need help from their parents if they are to prepare to be swimmers.

Our experience in camp shows us that children usually like something if they are good in it, and they can't be good at it

64

Camp Chicopi. College boys from Oklahoma Swim, both National
finalists, help younger boys

Breast-stroke champions Bonnie Benson (Canada) and Susan Rogers
(U.S.) take off for a set of push-off repeats at Mrs Dawson's camp

Mrs Dawson's daughter Marilyn, a Canadian National Age-Group record holder (14) dives into the Camp's home-made 50-metres pool

unless they work at developing the skill level required for excellence. Once they excel, they become leaders. We don't give lectures on Leadership, we teach skills that produce Leadership. In most cases, a young child does not have the interest span to work this hard without some help. A child will not develop his, or her, own unconditional commitment until the teens. Come the teens, and this commitment will be 'going steady', or 'hot rods' or 'rock and roll', nothing better unless the child is well on the way before his or her age of self-commitment. The urging and coaxing of a parent while still in unimpeachable authority is necessary in the pre-teen stages of such development. This sort of push can be quite firm, or quite subtle, depending on the child. There is an age of response, and an age of rebellion. We must back, and even 'push', our children during the age of response so they will have their own unconditional commitment during the age of rebellion. We do want them to have swimming in their teens, however, so do not press your luck too soon. This is not to be construed as an open licence to drive your child at a very early age, and we must ever be conscious of the individual child.

Many of us now feel that age-group swimming in the 10 and under division has drawbacks when it is over-emphasized. Teach the skills at this age, and ration competition to keep them hungry for more later on during the self-conscious age. It is most difficult to wait. Those of us interested in the team, team scores, etc. know that the 10 and under, or 8 and under points count just as much as 15–16–17 points. Pushing the younger children will drive many out of swimming before they ever get to the age of unconditional commitment. At this later age, the very monotony can be a wonderful anaesthetic to preoccupation with other teenage troubles. I believe tough interval training should not begin, in most cases, until the girl is 11 or 12, and the boy 12 or 13. The parent who is ambitious for an 8-year-old must be extremely clever if the child's interest is to be maintained, and not develop into rebellion before the age of self styled unconditional commitment has arrived.

We coaches interested in senior swimming will not play around with high pressure swimming for younger age groups unless our parent organization forces it upon us.

Parent organizations, like individual parents, are both good and the bad. Again, I believe they are usually much more good than bad. We need them for financial support, for timing at the contests, for transportation, and for a dozen other assorted details. We also need their moral backing with each individual child, and with the team as a whole. The coach can certainly maintain more authority if the parent-child bickering, cajoling, etc. is handled at home. Home is the place from which the trainer-parent must control eating and sleeping habits, and social life, and, more directly, must see that the swimmer gets down to the pool on time so the coach can take over. This is the parents' place in swimming, and not out on the deck during practice, or 'second guessing' the coach at contests. The parent who will not push his child out the door, or drive him to the pool, is much more of a problem for the age-group swim coach than the parent who pushes too hard. Let your child quit something he really wants to do and he'll resent it later. Until the child is old enough to become dedicated, he needs a parent to be dedicated for him. That his parent is living vicariously is no crime – all good parents do some vicarious living, and a parent who kicked his own opportunities in the teeth when young may want something better for his youngsters. The motives of parents are mixed. We should concern ourselves more with the effect on the child than the motive of the parent. Again, going to my camp experience, I find that almost all young children like to be told what to do. The teenagers, who may resent it, must be prepared so that they will have a worthwhile commitment before resentment comes.

Even when swimmers go away to college and quit, it is not necessarily the fault of the parent. Once on their own, they can not, or will not continue. Even in these cases where there was no personal commitment to swimming, I cannot say the parents were wrong. The swimming was a good thing while it lasted, and it never would have started, or reached any level of accomplishment, without that 'typical age-group parent', who knew when a pat on the back was best, and when a boot in the tail was best for his own particular child. Unconditional commitment will not always follow a good early push, but it will almost never come without such a push.

There are a couple of other plusses that Age-Group parents have brought into swimming. Age-Group has brought a great many very high quality adults into amateur sports. These wealthy, energetic, and talented, people came into swimming only because of their children and, once hooked, many stayed on to serve as volunteer sports committeemen, contest officials, fund-raisers, planners, and in many other necessary promotional capacities, sometimes long after their children grow up. The last three U.S. National Championship contests, and the Olympic trials, were each initiated, organized, and financed, through the efforts of men first interested in swimming as age-group fathers.

Olympic Coach, Jim Counsilman, feels the calibre of officiating will improve all over the world as age-group catches on. Because of the tremendous number of age-group meets, a great many people in the United States are not only experienced at timing and judging but they get a lot of practice and they are up on the rules. 'The officiating at the Olympics is often less than expected,' Dr Counsilman says, 'because many of the officials work a swimming contest only once every four years.'

12

How Various Coaches Handle Parents –
The Percentage of Success – Teaching or
Training and Other Matters

In spite of my last chapter defending the age-group parent, there are problems. Many coaches have expressed the opinion that the only ideal age-group coaching job would be at the Orphans' Home. We had no particular parent problems in my Ann Arbor Swim Club, only because we had no parents' organization. This worked fine in Ann Arbor, where we had an abundance of coaches and ex-swimmers; college graduate students, and undergraduates, to officiate and run the contests and to help my husband and me run the club, but this is not the case where a parent-organization is needed to finance and administer a swimming club. For this reason, I interviewed several outstanding age-group coaches to get their observations on how they handle the parents who pay their salary. In every case they acknowledged a parent problem, but they also volunteered that the parents' fundamental desire is the same as the coaches, better performance. With this common interest, there are very few differences that cannot be resolved.

Frank Elm, the New Jersey Coach, who put Phil Riker, Ginny Dunkel, and Sue Pitt, in the 1964 U.S. Olympic team, has one day a week set aside as 'parents' day'. He believes parents have a right to see their children practise so long as they do not bring a stop-watch, but parents in the stands are disturbing to the coach-swimmer concentration so he limits parents to 'visitors' day', much as I found we had to do at summer camp some years ago. The camp routine is interrupted when parents come, and so is a swim practice. Triangles seldom work as well as direct line communications and the idea that a coach should approach the children through their parents will not work. A coach is like an Army General or should be. He can ask a parent for advice and ask their help in handling a youngster but he does not have to ask. He should always be Supreme Commander in the swimming-pool, age-group as well as senior and college swimming.

Frank Elm tells the story about George Haines who kept hearing the click of watches at a practice until it began to annoy him. Haines collected all the watches, and checked them in a box outside the pool, then announced that parents could come and visit any time so long as they leave their watches, and do not talk to their children during practice.

'Red' Hucht, coach of the nationally ranked Baltimore K.C. Orchards team, has a direct approach for parents who give him suggestions on how to handle their children at practice. 'Ok. Bud,' he says 'you go coach them, then I'll have more time for those who want my coaching'.

Bob Ousley, Pompono Beach, Florida coach of John Nelson, the youngest 1964 male Olympic medal winner, likes to give the parents jobs helping the swimming club, but jobs removed from coaching responsibility, jobs that will help them mature as swimmer' parents. He thinks it unfair to parents to include them in coaching decisions although he agrees that they should be kept informed after his coaching decisions.

Jack Nelson, 1956 butterfly finalist at Melbourne, and present coach of the Fort Lauderdale Swimming Association team, has a parent committee appointed by himself, 'a few special parents who agreed with me'. These parents handle parent situations for him. Nelson says he can look back, and not too far back, to see that young coaches, as well as young-to-swimming parents, need maturing. The combination of immaturity in both is just 'too much', according to Nelson.

All coaches agree that parents are a necessary evil to age-group swimming, and not always evil, and never all evil. The coach is always fighting numerical odds with his age-group swimmers. He cannot tell which ones will stay interested, which will respond to his coaching, which ones will work, and grow, and develop skill, and talent. Very few will reach the top. The coach knows he will lose a large percentage of his swimmers before maturity, but the parent with only one prospect in his family puts all his hopes in one swimmer and blames the coach if things go wrong. It is difficult for a man with only one swimmer to play the percentages.

Jack Nelson says the reason we lose most of our girls at 15 and 16 is because their minds go bad, swimming-wise, and for no other reason. This seems to be a U.S. phenomena. We just do not have any Dawn Frasers. Nelson says age-group must not only get the children into swimming but figure out how to keep them in it until maturity. The college coaches who complain that age-groupers start too young, and quit too young, would not want these quitters anyway according to Nelson. This is a large order for everybody concerned, swimmer, coach, and parent. Nelson has a boy who quit after winning national ranking as a 10 and under, then started again at 15. This boy says he quit because he had already won the medals, and trips, and that neither he nor his parents saw any percentage in gambling on future competition. He drifted out of swimming, but missed it, and came back and loves it, and wishes he never had dropped out. This boy believes he, and others like him, lose a great deal dropping out, and that comebacks like his are a rarity. He is one of the few who has quit, and then can come back to advise others not to quit.

Bob Mowerson, who put butterflyer Walt Richardson and breast-stroker Virgil Luken in the 1964 U.S. Olympic team, has been a college coach for 8 years (Minnesota and Michigan State) and a high school coach for 18 years at Battle Creek, Michigan. Mowerson says the difference between an age-group, or high school coach, and a college coach, is the difference between a teacher and a trainer. Every coach is a bit of both, but an age-group coach should be a teacher whereas senior swimmers often cannot be taught and need a trainer. The late Matt Mann used to say, 'Give me a college boy who has already done a lot of swimming and the first fault I try to correct in his Freshman year will be the last fault I'm still correcting when he graduates 4 years later'. Age-group coaches have an obligation to teach good swimming techniques in the formative swimming years. This should be number one, whereas college coaches, or club senior coaches, must concentrate on conditioning in order to get maximum effort from the talent they inherit from age-group. Mowerson, having done both kinds of coaching, wishes coaches at each level would define and accept their role as teachers, or trainers, giving credit for those swimmers who others have taught or those swimmers who others will train.

70

My father, Matt Mann, used to say, 'there is always room at the top because many are called but few are chosen'. It takes a very special combination of skill, desire, and circumstances, to hit the top in an Olympic year, or any other year. Be it age-group or senior, a coach or coaches are usually better qualified than parents to get this special combination out of most youngsters.

And, finally, as Dr Jim Counsilman says: 'The parents are there to help the coach and not to run the organisation.'

13

A Dozen Do's and Don't's on Meet Behaviour for Age-Group Parents

One of the great beauties of age-group swimming is the way it brings families together in an interest that is primarily a child interest but also a vehicle for parent-effort with and for the children. Age-group is togetherness, an excuse for the family to go away on week-end trips, an activity in which the child, or children, he and/or she, are featured but know that mother and father are also a necessity as timers, chauffeurs, etc. Since this is an activity in which you, as parents, share in your children's activity there is a daily dozen for you to remember.

1. *Never* time the lane in which your child is swimming. Excuse yourself, and find a substitute timer for that particular race.
2. *Never* judge a race in which your child is one of the contestants.
3. *Never* argue with an official. Leave this to your coach, and do not badger the coach to argue a decision affecting your team and particularly your child.
4. *Never* pester your coach with details, or complaints, during the course of a contest. He is under pressure enough running the team.
5. *Never* ask for special privileges, especially on trips. Your child should sleep and eat with the team if there are accommodations.
6. *Never* discuss your ideas on technique with, or in front of, the children, and don't chase windmills. There is no one right way to swim any stroke, or any race, so do not tell your coach how some other coach does it.
7. *Always* ask if your team needs drivers or officials (most teams usually do) but do not be too insistent, particularly if your child is embarrassed, and most children are embarrassed by their parents at one time or another. If your coach

needs you to drive, or officiate, and your child says 'No', then it is up to the coach to intercede and explain his needs to the swimmers. His endorsement can often win you new respect from your children. At any rate, do not be loud or over juvenile. Leave the fight-songs and formal cheers to the children.

8. *Never* 'second guess' your coach. If something sticks in your gullet, see him privately, or take it through channels. A coach usually must keep his own counsel. If you do not like his methods, fire him at the annual meeting but, once re-hired, he has to be the boss of the team. There is no other way to have a good team.

9. Unless you are an official, *always* stay away from the deck at contests and particularly at practice.

10. *Always* make sure your children dress appropriately, and act like ladies and gentlemen. Have the coach, or group, set up the rules for behaviour in advance, and then insist that your children comply.

11. *Always* make sure your children have adequate spending money and don't have to cadge off other parents or the coach.

12. *Always* see that your child limits his or her luggage on a trip.

In addition to the dozen do's and don'ts of meet behaviour there are two more don'ts for after the meet. Don't take a stop-watch to practice, and don't sit in the stands to time your child *unless* you have one of the few coaches in the world who does not mind this. You cannot hear the coach's instructions – any of dozens of factors may be more important to him in a single practice than the time. If coach has asked your son or daughter to slow down and concentrate on a stroke change, your stop-watch can be most disconcerting.

Do not ask your coach 'What do you think my young son's chances are of becoming great?' He does not know.

14

Operation Mexico

THE U.S.A. NEEDS A NATIONAL AGE-GROUP CHAMPIONSHIP CONTEST

In California, where age-group has been most successful in the United States, it is the consensus of coaches and officials that age-group swimmers should not travel outside their home geographical districts for contests, that such glamorous travel be reserved for senior swimming. There are several reasons for this view; tiring trips for the very young, exposure to social experiences before they are ready, the education of the public to a tolerance and acceptance of competitive sports, and expense. The biggest reason in the perspective aimed at Olympic development is that the glamour of travel should be rationed so that it will be a plum to offer seniors working hard for national and international trips. The child who has already been everywhere, worn all the uniforms, and won all the medals, is not so likely to work as hard again, and again, and again, and may not put in the big effort for the big events. Success can come too soon, and too often, at least this is the experience and the opinion in California, and in the U.S. National AAU Committee, where such things are discussed. The people interested in mature athletes winning national and international games, want a gradual increase in effort, and commensurate reward culminating in the Olympic games.

This discussion is necessary because of abuses developing in new areas that think they are emulating the American age-group success story. Because of the great parent interest in promoting their small children, there are countries which hire planes, buy uniforms, and fly national age-group teams to international age-group games, using up both the budget and the interest which might later support senior competitions. The standard excuse is, 'swimming in our country is not yet ready for open competition, so the age-group programme *is* more important *now*. The trouble is that both parents, and children, have had their trips, their titles, their success, and the novelty is gone when you ask them to contribute a much greater expenditure of time, money, and desire, later on. There is a desire for premature retirement with laurels intact rather than to go back for more at greater odds. Father has had it, and Junior is relieved to retire without any more pressure at the breakfast table. This is my point of view, but it is not unanimous as evidenced by Barbara Harvey's letter, and by Carl Bauer's remarks, both published in this book.

My point is not to pick a quarrel but to suggest alternatives that will put age-group sports in perspective, and still keep them fun for father and son.

In the United States, there is no National Age-Group Contest because of the great distance children would be required to travel, and because coaches want to save the reward of this national trip for swimmers who can make the senior nationals in open competition. The incentive is for younger swimmers to try to graduate out of age classifications into open events, rather than for older teenagers to try to hang on in the top age-group classifications. This is at least one of the reasons why the U.S. Nationals (Senior) and the U.S. Olympic team, include so many 14- to 17-year-old swimmers who want to be 'the best' rather than 'the best junior' or 'the best of my age'.

In order to set a standard of excellence, the National Age-Group Committee keeps national records, and publishes annual lists, of the five best age-group times in each event. This gives a champion in any local area an idea of where he really stands, but several abuses also show up in this. Until 1963, the times had to be established in an age-group contest which meant a 14-year-old was obliged to swim in the age classification to get top rating, even though she might be beating all comers in better time. This discouraged age-groupers from swimming 'open' when ready, and it set up a false rating whereby the best of a given age was not necessarily the champion. An outstanding champion who had 'ducked' the open races could replace her. In 1961, for example, Jean Ann Dellekamp was U.S. National Champion in the 100 yds breaststroke, but rated 4th in age-group. Everyone knew her age, but she could not be listed among

75

the five best times because her swimming had not been in events specifically restricted to her 13–14 age-group.

This abuse has been corrected, and the validity of age-group records and ratings improved by the correction. There was another abuse called 'birthday time trials', and still another was the practice of seeking out a 20 yd or a 50 yd pool to try for a record in an event seldom contested, because fewer people swim in those length pools. Some of these abuses are inevitable, but the National and Regional AAU Association Swim Committees are constantly trying to improve the situation. In the meantime, age-group does interest vast numbers of parents, expose thousands of children to competitive swimming, and feed specially talented children into the big time. Record-conscious newspapermen give swimming much needed publicity, even if the honour sometimes goes to the wrong age competitor.

There is an alternative that will give the youngsters competition to whet their appetite without jading them to the glamour of travel, and that will offer a truly national or international age-group championship without the abuses of ratings. In Canada, they name it after the upcoming Olympics – Operation Tokyo became Operation Mexico right after the Tokyo Olympic games. Here is how it works in Canada, and how it would work anywhere by mail, telegraph, telephone or radio. Obviously, smaller dual contests between countries can also be telegraphed without the necessity of wide travel for youngsters.

Canada's Operation Tokyo was, and is, a National Age-Group Championship Contest. Each principal swimming area in Canada holds an age-group contest on the same day and the results are wired, or telphoned, to Montreal where electronic computers tabulate the results and send them out by telephone, radio, and press wire within minutes. During the course of the Provincial contests, results of earlier races are read off, indicating both national and local ratings.

The U.S.A. is long overdue on such an arrangement in place of, or in addition to, the controversial age-group ratings which label 690 champions. We could pick a set week-end each winter, and another each summer, as Indoor or Outdoor *National Age-Group Swimming Days*. The AAU Associations would each hold an age-group championship two-day contest, the same contest and orders of events in all Associations. The Association results would be locally honoured as State or Association Age-Group Championships, and the national results of the top ten in each event would also be published. Complete results, or the first one hundred in each event, could be published in pamphlet form for circulation later.

Such a National Age-Group Championship would do away with the travel problems of the senior national contests, would provide for an exciting single week-end climax to age-group seasons, would mean that all swimmers would be swimming under near equal conditions, would cut down on the number of events recognized as national events, put age-group swimming back on a seasonal basis, eliminate local timing scandals, time trial records, and many other abuses of the present rating system and it would be far better than the proposed regional age-group Championships combining associations for more of the young swimmer travel abuses California and others have worked so long to eliminate.

It would, in fact, bring age-group swimming of age with appropriate National Championships and without travel.

Canada does not have swimmers such as we have in America, but in Operation Tokyo, now Operation Mexico, they do have a truly National Age-Group Swimming Championship with national public interest, recognition and a much more honest and simple way of rating swimmers. Any national age-group record set in this contest, under pre-ordained uniform standards of timing and officiating, could be accepted on the confirmed results without the complicated form-filling now required. These championship records would be acceptable to many who doubt the validity of some of our present age-group standards. National news stories would credit these age-group performances.

With such a meet, Harold Heller and his association age-group chairmen can keep their hair and their sanity, not for ever, but a bit longer.

And, while we are at it, such a national telegraphic championship would be a good idea for the 50 high school state meets too. It would certainly eliminate some of the controversy in the selection of the mass high school All-American teams.

15

A Bit of Age-Group Swimming History

The U.S. Age-Group Swimming Programme began in 1953 in California, and the 1960 Olympics were the first Games to feel its impact. The following story traces those beginnings through a few California girls, the first who grew up in age-group to make an Olympic team.

After the United States had surprised a favoured Australian team by completely dominating both men's and women's swimming at the 1960 (Rome) Olympics, reporters asked U.S. Coach, Gus Stager, what was the reason for the tremendous upsurge in U.S. swimming. 'Age-Group!' said Stager, and Women's Olympic Coach George Haines agreed. So what is 'Age-Group'?

Age-Group swimming is a U.S. National sports craze, yet it started only in 1953. There are 500,000 youngsters in this fast growing programme first organized on a large scale in California under Beth Kaufman, the Amateur Athletic Union's retired national age-group swimming chairman. Age-group was the brainchild of Carl Bauer of the Missouri Athletic Club in Saint Louis, who felt that young swimmers needed a national development programme of races requiring them to swim against other children their own ages. Bauer began introducing his idea of carefully regulated swimming races for boys and girls in four age-groups, 10 and under, 11–12, 13–14, 15–16, at the 1949 AAU Convention. He was shouted down with cries of 'That's too young'. 'Parents won't stand for it.' 'How can it be controlled?' 'They'll all lie about their ages.' 'There's plenty of swimming, and we don't bar those kids now.'

By 1951, the idea had won enough friends for a trial run, with California the test area. It was an instant success and, by 1953, it was adopted on a national scale with Mrs Kaufman, a former California Red Cross official, as chairman. In 1965, a little more than 11 years after age-group went national, there were 44 states or AAU associations with year-round age-group programmes and Kellum Johnson, swim conscious ex-National AAU President, estimated there were 500,000 young swimmers competing in what he called 'quite the biggest thing the AAU has undertaken'. The AAU is the governing body of 11 Olympic sports in the United States.

The contrast between age-group and pre age-group in U.S. swimming is dramatically illustrated by two recent swimming incidents, one at Louisville, and one at Berea, Kentucky, The Louisville story was told to me at the National AAU convention in Chicago by Jack Thompson, and Col. Ralph Wright of the Plantation Swim Club. Thompson was running a large age-group meet that summer when he noticed something peculiar happening in the boys' 10 and under 50-mtr freestyle race. The boy in the lead suddenly stopped, shook himself in the water, reached back to his feet for something, and then continued swimming, but awkwardly. He seemed to be dragging his left arm. Thompson was worried that the boy had a cramp, but the roar of laughter which broke out in the audience indicated it was something less serious. As the boy approached the finish line, the contest director saw that he had lost his trunks and was holding them in his left hand. His embarrassed mother ran from the stands with a blanket and tried to surround him with it as he climbed out of the water. 'Why didn't you stop when you lost your suit?' she scolded, and the little boy began to cry. 'You just don't understand, Ma, he said. 'We needed the points; a guy just can't quit in the middle of a race!' The crowd clapped and cheered as the mother bundled her son off to the locker room.

Oscar Gunkler, physical education director and swim coach at Berea College, about fifty miles east of Louisville, is a strong believer in age-group swimming, even though his area has yet to experience it. 'Berea is a college which essentially draws from eleven hill counties,' he says, 'and most of these students have never had a coach or even a pool to swim in, but we have a fine pool at the college. We require every student to pass a swimming test before graduation.'

One autumn recently, Gunkler was classifying a group of incoming freshmen on their swimming ability when a large mountaineer jumped into the pool, thrashed and spluttered, and began to sink. Gunkler grabbed him. 'What's the matter, son,' he asked, 'can't you swim?'

'Don't know, Professor,' the boy gasped. 'I ain't never tried it.'

'The boy learned to swim,' Gunkler says, 'and so do all our students, but they learn just about ten years too late for us to produce any champion swimming teams at Berea.'

It was the view of our successful past Olympic swimming coaches, Bob Kiphuth (1948) and Matt Mann (1952) that the only way we could regain the swimming Olympic supremacy we lost to the Australians in 1956 was to start our swimmers young, and keep them at it. The 1960 team, under coach Gus Stager, proved this point, winning with a team dominated by present and past age-group swimming champions.

The late Matt Mann, the dean of active U.S. swimming coaches, and for 50 years one of the most successful, when he died in harness at 78, always practised this through his children's summer camps in Northern Ontario. Twenty Olympic swimmers, and more than two hundred All-Americans, have come out of these camps, with many of them beginning as eight- or ten-year-old non-swimmers. For a long time, swimming was not a universal sport, and Matt Mann had a reasonable chance of developing a national champion out of any able-bodied boy or girl who started young enough and stuck with it. Matt was still turning out champion swimmers when he died a few years ago, but the rest of the world was catching up with him. Age-group has changed things by bringing swimming to masses of eager youngsters throughout the United States.

Whereas Mann started with a base of 75 summer campers, the Riviera Club of Indianapolis, coached by Gene Lee, teaches 2,000 boys and girls to swim each summer, and another 1,500 in the winter programme. Becky Collins was a graduate of these beginner groups (class of 1952) and with 3,500 children each year in the club's learn-to-swim programme, there are sure to be other Beckys' on the way up. This mass exposure to swimming is the secret of Riviera's success, and to keep the children interested in going on with the sport, the club is dedicated to age-group swimming races with other boys and girls their ages until they get old enough, big and skilfull enough to swim with the Riviera 'varsity in open competition.

Becky Collins, like all other U.S. age-group swimmers, could not have become a champion without a coach, a pool to swim in, the will to win, and dedicated family backing. There is no magic formula except persistence and hard work.

When Becky was ten, her mother began driving her to Riviera for summer lessons in one of the club's three outdoor pools. 'I wasn't sure I liked it at first,' the young champion now says, 'but Mama said I'd have to finish what I'd started, and stay with it at least for the summer. She came with me every day, and then when I learned to swim I decided I'd like to go and swim some more.'

There are a great many children who have used the wonderful sport of age-group swimming to overcome physical and emotional handicaps, but Becky is not one of them. She comes from an uncomplicated middle western, middle class, middle income, American family that backs her up as you would expect a family to back a dedicated child in any worthwhile ambition. This former Riviera and I.A.C. swimmer, now retired, was able to swim because her father, a wiry, hard-bitten old newspaper man, was willing to put up with 'oven meals' at irregular hours to fit his daughter's practice schedule, and because her mother had the patience to sit long hours by the pool while her daughter swam.

There is one other important factor – cost. Becky's swimming fees when she was at Riviera were only $10.00 yearly. 'Volume is our answer,' said the late Riviera coach, Johnny Galvich, 'We run a glorified baby-sitting programme so that more kids can get the chance to swim. And there is something in it for everyone. We are proudest of the great number of kids we teach to swim. If they want to keep on with it, we will, of course, keep on with them, and eventually, after a few years, we may get a champion. It works rather like a tube of toothpaste. You keep stuffing them in the bottom, and something is bound to squirt out the top sooner or later. Anyhow, toothpaste leaves a nice, clean taste in your mouth, and so does teaching children to swim.

Riviera is a family club with 5,000 families, but no bar. The club's founder, the late James Makin, included uncles, cousins, and grandchildren, in his conception of a family unit. It costs $100 for a family to join, but, after joining, it costs only $10.00

a year per person. There are basketball and tennis courts, bowling, dances, and card parties, but the main activity is swimming.

Riviera is currently one of the most successful age-group swimming teams in the United States, but on a more modest scale the Riviera formula of mass low-cost participation in swimming is now being multiplied all over the country in co-operative and community-owned pools. This ability to afford swimming as a family activity is what is making age-group the U.S.A.'s fastest growing children's sport.

In Beth Kaufman's Pacific Association (California, Monterey and north) there are more than 2,700 registered AAU card-carrying swimmers, and in the Southern California Association, during a twelve-month period, there were more than 22,000 age-group swimming contest entries. 'It has made our youth swimming conscious,' says Mrs Kaufman proudly, 'and it has made California a swimming leader. Ridiculous as it may seem, with our climate, this was not so until age-group began catching on just a few years ago.'

Perhaps the first great champion to come exclusively from California age-group was Sylvia Ruuska. 'The Ruuska story, like most age-group successes, is strictly a family tale,' Beth Kaufman told me, 'I'll never forget them at a meeting I was helping to officiate at Russian River. "Giddy yup! Giddy yup! Giddy yup, Sylvia! Giddy yup, Mama!" You could have heard Papa Ruuska two countries away. He was the coach, but he liked to sit up in the stands during a contest. He says if his team was not coached enough before they got there, it was not going to help for him to be down there coaching them between races.

'In the Russian River contest, Ruuska's Berkley team had two relay teams. The "A" team was anchored by 11-year-old Sylvia Ruuska, and the "B" team by her mother. The old man kept "Giddy yupping!" from the stands, and Sylvia won easily. I was at the finish line and tried to congratulate her,' says Beth Kaufman. 'She climbed out of the pool and ran right by me over to another lane where her mother was still swimming. "Come on, Mama, hurry, Mama, hurry!" she pleaded, and Mrs Ruuska, exhausted, brought her relay in third. Papa Ruuska was down out of the stands, and Mama's family crowded around to pound her on the back, and hug the breath out of her – the little bit she had left. Berkley won the meet easily, and Sylvia's relay set a record, but the whole family was more excited about Mama bringing the "B" relay in third.'

Sylvia Ruuska is also an old lady now, by modern swimming standards, as she must be only five years younger than Dawn Fraser. She made the 1956 Olympic team at 13, and two years later went to Australia where she set world's swimming records in the 1,500-mtrs and 400-mtrs individual medley. She won four events in 1958 to win the high point trophy at the Women's Nationals in Topeka, Kansas, and she was captain of the Women's Olympic team in 1960. She retired after the Olympics in 1960.

'There is no question,' Beth Kaufman said, as she introduced me to Sylvia Ruuska's father at the Women's Indoor Nationals at West Palm Beach, Florida, in 1959, 'that this man has the number one family in age-group swimming. They've been in it from the start.'

Ruuska was deeply involved in the Nationals, and I knew he would be busy, but I certainly wanted an interview. He put his hand on my shoulder, and tried to interest me in an hour of surf riding at 6 a.m. 'I do it every morning,' he said. 'It's great.'

'I have another appointment for breakfast,' I lied, and we agreed to meet at the pool at 10 a.m. Next morning we met as scheduled.

'Mama couldn't come with us,' he apologized. 'I don't like to come to these things without her, but someone has to stay at home and coach the rest of our team.'

I asked about his team and their training. 'We work hard,' he said. 'That's our only secret. We swim in the Berkely YMCA pool. It's a 20 yd pool, and it is narrow, but it's water, and we are very grateful. We have to swim a pattern to get everyone in, two circles with the boys using one side of the pool, and the girls the other. You cannot practise slow to swim fast, so the good ones have to swim around the slower ones. Sometimes, that passing gets pretty rough. We limit our 'varsity to 30, 15 boys and 15 girls. It's still very crowded. There's a waiting list of 200. My wife teaches two Y swim classes, and we get our 'varsity swimmers out of the classes. It's just like everyone else except we have a small pool and very little pool time.'

'Isn't there a 25-yds regulation pool anywhere in Berkley?' I asked.

'Oh, yes,' he said. 'Berkley High School has two fine pools, but it would take an act of Congress to get in one. They act as if they are afraid we'd contaminate the water.'

Knowing the prevailing trend in coaching swimmers is two or three work-outs a day, I asked Ruuska how he managed this. 'We don't,' he said. 'There are a lot of people who must use the Y pool, and we can get it only in the evening for an hour and one-half. Then we have our swimmers run two miles before school in the morning. Most coaches think this is crazy, especially during the season, but I'm an electrician. I'm just an amateur coach, and don't know any better, so I run them all season long. Sure, it would be better if we had a big pool, and a chance to swim more often, but I think I'd still run them. My girls don't become exhausted on the 400 individual medley like so many do, and I think it is because they run.

'Too many swimmers save up on that race. You must swim all four strokes all out if you expect to win it.'

Perhaps Ruuska was building me up for the race that was about to start. Both his daughters were in the final of seven. The race needed no build-up. It was the best race in a championship in which seven records were equalled or broken. For sixteen lengths, four of each stroke (butterfly, back, breast, and freestyle) the Ruuska girls and Becky Collins battled it out. In the preliminaries, Sylvia Ruuska broke her championship record of five minutes, three and five-tenths seconds; then, in a later heat, Miss Collins broke Sylvia's new record. In the thrilling final, Sylvia and Becky both broke five minutes, the first time any girl swimmer in the world had done so. Sylvia won in 4:58.2 and Becky was second in 4:58.5. Pat Ruuska was third, just a few seconds over the magic five minute mark which had stood as a mental and physical barrier, like the four-minute mile stood so long in track. Sylvia Ruuska, who had set nine world records in the six months just preceding those Nationals, was finally pressed to her greatest effort, and by a younger girl who, like herself, swam to the top out of America's new age-group swimming craze. The two girls tied for high point score at the Nationals with 22 points each. 'And that's the way it is going to be,' said Weikko Ruuska. 'Age- Group is going to push all our champions, and pull our records down to the point where we'll beat the Australians and anybody else who wants to swim us.'

Self-confident coach Ruuska had refused to be embroiled in a coaches' discussion about the eligibility of several girls swimming with the University of Houston team. 'Why should I ?' he asked. 'We'll win anyway, whether they swim or not.' To try for the National AAU team championships, he brought just four girls, and they won with 78 points in spite of a mild case of food poisoning which kept two of the girls (Ann Bancroft and Carolyn Schuler) up all night, the night before the contest started. 'That had me worried,' Ruuska said. 'It must have been the salad-dressing. I would like to bring more girls if we had the money, but four is all you need, if they are good enough.'

Ruuska's four swimmers won both relays, two other first places, and place points in all but three swimming events to win the contest over Houston's College girls by 27 points. With one or two exceptions, Ruuska grew his own swimmers through age-group, starting them at 8 or 10 years of age in local meets. When I went to congratulate him on his remarkable feat of winning the Women's Nationals with just four swimmers, Ruuska reminded me of the many years, and the many swimmers who started out in age-group, that it took to give him those four. 'And don't you forget, young lady,' he said, using his big index finger to emphasize the point, 'don't you forget that the biggest thing about age-group is that it is a family affair. My hobby costs me money, but if it wasn't for age-group swimming I'd be off doing something else instead of working with my kids in all my spare time.' And Ruuska was right about that, too. As an amateur coach he stayed in the game only as long as his daughters swam. The whole family has now retired from swimming. This is perhaps one of the shortcomings in this great new sports fad. Parent coaches are often in it only as long as their children swim.

Contrasted with Papa Ruuska and his booming voice was another swimming father I met at the National Championships – suave, mild-mannered Alex Kempner, from Beverly Hills, California. Kempner, a slight, balding man, has nothing in common with Ruuska, except that they both gave their all-out support to dedicated swimming daughters. Patty Kempner, a bit less than a year younger than record-holder Sylvia, was, like her rival, a senior national record-holder who rewrote the age-group record books on her climb up the swimming ladder, and polished off her career by making the 1960 Olympic team.

Patty was the star of the Kris Kristenson swimming school which tied Berkley for second in the 1958 Indoor Nationals at Dallas. Kris Kristenson, who coached the winning U.S.A. girls' Pan-American swimming team in 1959, preferred to let Mr Kempner speak for them both. Kempner was shy, but not reluctant. He is proud of his daughter, and thinks swimming has given her a great deal. Patty is neither tall like Sylvia Ruuska, nor tiny like Becky Collins. She is medium height, and slightly on the plump side, which demonstrates that there is no particular size, weight or physical type that makes the ideal swimmer.

'She started at the age of six,' he father told me. 'When she was 13, I took her to the Olympic trials in Detroit in 1956. She had never been out of age-group before, and when I walked into the pool with her, I felt as if I was bringing the left fielder on Hollywood High to the Yankee training camp. To my amazement, all the champions from all over the country, whom she had never met, knew her from the records she had made in age-group. She qualified for the finals of the 200 mtrs breast, and finished fifth.

'When she was 10,' Mr Kempner added, 'Patty swam a backstroke 50 yd race at Palm Springs. The race in the finals was between Sylvia Ruuska and Patty, as they were far ahead of the field. They hit the wall together for the turn, and Sylvia came up in Patty's lane. Sylvia won. I was the referee of the meet, and my stroke and turn judge came up with a disqualification that I was reluctant to accept, as my child was involved. The judge went to Patty, and asked her whether Sylvia had interfered with her. Patty said, no, she didn't even know Sylvia was there (a lie if I ever heard one) and begged that she should not be disqualified. It is sportsmanship of this kind that is instilled in these age-group kids from an early age. I was far prouder of Patty for this, than if she had won the race.

'Patty has understood the score since she was a very little

girl,' her father says. 'She knows that she is a dedicated child, as are all the top swimmers in age-group. There is no getting away from the fact that they make considerable sacrifices to succeed. The long hours devoted to practice, especially during the school year, when they come home late and tired to their homework, fall asleep over it, and get up at the crack of dawn the next morning to finish it before school. The many social activities, parties, etc., that they are obliged to pass up because they interfere with their swimming activities. The summer season when they see their friends go off to beach parties and picture shows, for pleasure bent, while they must go to swimming practice. I think that you should not gloss over this side of the picture, but rather bring out the fact that the kids realize all this, and gladly make the sacrifice for the sake of the rewards.

'Patty goes to a Catholic School – Marymount – and the nuns are 100 per cent in favour of her swimming activities,' her father told me. 'They feel that age-group is the finest antidote for juvenile delinquency that there is. When she goes to a National, they pray for her.'

Just exactly why is this age-group swimming so worthwhile? I found the answer to this question varies in accordance with the person being questioned. 'It is important to professional coaches,' says Houston coach Phill Hansel, President of the American Swimming Coaches' Association, 'because it has put swimming before the masses, and made it a major sport in high school and college.'

'In our area,' says the Santa Clara Swim Club and 1960 Women's Olympic coach, George Haines, 'we had three high school swimming teams when the age-group programme went national eight years ago, and now we have dozens.'

Gus Stager, coach of the University of Michigan, and the 1960 Men's Olympic Coach, says, 'You can notice the improvement in swimmers coming to college every year. Age-group has taught swimmers to work. A freshman now doesn't even blink an eye the first time I tell him to get in and swim 100 lengths. Thanks to age-group, the good swimmers are well on the way before they even get to high school, and certainly before they get to college. It has forced the college coaches to give these swimmers the specialized training they deserve.'

'It has broadened the base of our national swimming

pyramid,' says George Wendler, a swimming parent whose son and daughter have been moderately successful team swimmers with the Detroit Turners Athletic Club. 'Age-group has given competitive swimming to the masses where it was, until very recently, the privilege of the boy wealthy enough to belong to a private athletic club.'

'If the country really wants fitness,' says Ray Daughters, past chairman of the AAU and Olympic men's swimming Committee, 'then swimming is the best exercise there is, and age-group is the answer to complete exposure.' Daughters was the coach of butterfly swimmer Nancy Ramey, the first age-group swimmer to set a world record. Nancy retired as U.S. national champion in the 100-yds butterfly, and record-holder.

In one community, the Kraus-Weber test was given to all children within the 10–16 age brackets covered by the AAU age-group swimming programme. 100 per cent of the swimmers passed the test, while only 20 per cent of non-swimmers passed it. 'Through the programme, an ever increasing wave of healthy, better adjusted, physically fit, boys and girls are taking their places in the world,' according to the AAU's committee, assigned to evaluate the new sport's progress. 'These children have learned the discipline, respect for officials and valid regulations necessary to success in our competitive adult society. The programme, while growing in numbers, has remained local and de-emphasized where injurious pressures are involved, and yet has offered national recognition and local approval for meritorious achievement by its participants.'

Many recreation people question the national nature of the age-group programme, just as little league baseball is most frequently criticized for taking the boy too far away from home. Mrs Bime Close of the Dolphin Swim Club, Stamford, Connecticut, takes exception to this, and cites one of her swimmers as a case in point.

'12-year-old Carole Manaly was a consistent age-group winner in the butterfly stroke,' says Mrs Close, 'but her times were nowhere near a national level. I felt that Carole could do better. Winning, I told her, is often only a matter of who is competing in your race that particular day. We must try our very best every single time. Only the stop-watch can tell us how good we are.'

Carole kept winning in Connecticut and in New York City, and her times did not improve, so her coach sent her to a contest in age-group enthusiastic Philadelphia, where she finished among the also-rans. One week later, Carole won the 11–12 age 50 butterfly race in the Connecticut age-group championships, setting a new state record in her best time. After her new record was announced, she was presented with her trophy as Mrs Close asked her if she did not feel pretty good about all this, which showed that her swimming was improving. 'I don't know,' she said. 'I don't feel so hot . . . last week in Philadelphia with this same exact time, I was seventh.'

'Carole had learned,' says her coach, 'that winning is often only a matter of who happened to be competing that day, so that only the stop-watch can tell us how good we are.'

Beth Kaufman says the travel problem in age-group swimming is only temporary. 'The way this thing is growing,' she says, 'it soon won't be necessary for girls like Carole to travel so far to get competition.' In 1958, thirty-four states had year-round age-group programmes. 'More swimming-conscious people are demanding more and more community-owned pools, and these pools are giving swimming to more kids, who in turn demand still more swimming opportunity,' she says. 'In New York City area, for example, the number of registered swimmers went from 60 to 1,200 in the first eight years of age-group. In each age bracket the previous year's best performances are being broken.'

Phil Moriority, 1960 Olympic diving coach, and the Yale Swimming coach, feels that the most wonderful thing about age-group swimming is the way it involves parents in their children's activities. Phil runs the famous 'can' classes for faculty children at Yale (a tin can fastened to the back of a belt around the child's waist keeps him afloat while he learns to swim and does not interfere with his stroking the way a tube or life-jacket would) and is involved with a great deal of the AAU age-group swimming in the New England area. 'It takes a minimum of twenty-four timers, ten judges, three recorders, a starter, an announcer, and a referee, to run an outdoor eight lane age-group contest,' says Moriority. 'That is at least forty people, just to run a contest, and where are you going to get that many people unless you use parents?'

'In Little League Baseball,' says Beth Kaufman, 'the parents sit up in the stands and complain about the coaching and umpiring. The kids are embarrassed, and ask their folks not to come. In fact, age-group swimming is about the only teen and pre-teen activity I know where the kids really want their parents around. You cannot run a good swimming contest without the parents actually taking a working part, and the children know it, and are proud when Pop does a good job at the finish line, or Mom is a good turn judge.'

The only real problem is when the parent is more dedicated than the swimmer,' says Ockey Brunnell, father of Philadelphia's Frankie Brunnell, perhaps the outstanding eastern boy developed early in age-group swimming. 'I, for one, put too much importance on Frank's winning, and it caused many complications that could have been serious.' Mr Brunnell says that most of the mistakes made in age-group swimming are made by over-anxious parents. In Frank's case, his father feels that the boy got too much attention too young, and that he, the father, did not help him to keep swimming in its proper perspective. Both father and son can now talk freely about it, since Frank became a good student at Indiana University, swam better than ever, but also prepared for a solid future when his swimming was over.

'The Konrads, Australian world record-holders, took to swimming because they were polio victims,' says the late Matt Mann. 'Closer to home, Shelly Mann, U.S. Olympic gold medalist (1956) and world record-holder, was a post-polio. Every section of the country has some courageous child who is using his or her swimming to conquer polio, and gain athletic prominence that most children do not have the incentive to achieve.'

Perhaps the most courageous example in age-group swimming was Ellen Longo of Bellview, Nebraska. Ellen was one of six swimming brothers and sisters, and she was the best of them in spite of crippling polio which made her right leg useless from the age of two. The doctors said Ellen would never walk. Several operations were only partially successful, and in 1955 she began swimming. She wears a brace which she takes off just before she goes into the pool, and she hops to the starting blocks on her good left leg, but, once in the water, Ellen asks no quarter. In swimming, her right leg drags, and at the Phillips 66 age-group meet at Bartlesville, Oklahoma in 1957, she was disqualified in the butterfly stroke because her legs were not kicking together. After the referee learned the circumstances he reinstated her, and Ellen went on to take fifth in the finals. The next year she was second in the Nebraska state meet and she won most of her age-group races in the 11–12 year classification. 'Nothing seems too much for her. She has terrific drive and determination. It makes me proud to be a swimming coach when this sport gives someone like Ellen a chance to show her stuff,' says coach Bill O'Hearn.

'Of course there will be mistakes in age-group swimming,' said the late Matt Mann, who saw the whole sport of swimming grow up in his lifetime, 'but the good to hundreds of thousands of youngsters should not be sacrificed because of a few abuses.' Mann was the over-arm side-stroke champion of Great Britain before the turn of the century. He grew with his sport through the strictly athletic club phase and was this country's first full-time college coach. Over a fifty year span at Yale, Michigan, and Oklahoma, he won more national collegiate team titles than any other coach. 'This may give me the authority to speak on swimming,' he once said, 'but I want to point out the championships are never anything but the by-product. Swimming is a wonderful sport because it is the best competitive outlet I know for a child who is long on desire and short on natural ability. A track-man is either naturally fast, or he isn't going to be a runner, but no one knows how to swim until you teach him. It is an excellent body-building sport that does not require unusual co-ordination or ability. It requires hard work but, because of the natural buoyancy of the water, young swimmers don't seem to be able to strain themselves to the point of exhaustion as they often do in running races, or running games. Water is the great equalizer on natural ability. It is always there as resistance, but swimmers don't collapse at the finish of a race and there has never been a swimmer break a record who has not turned to his coach and said, "I believe I could have gone faster".

'There is no question in my mind but that swimming, through age-group, is the safest and most beneficial sports programme we have ever had for competitive-minded youngsters.

The most obvious testimony for swimming,' Mann said, 'is

the large number of handicapped children who have been helped physically and mentally.'

The 'swim for health' group who have become champions is not limited to polio cases. The celebrated Wardrop twins from Motherwell, Scotland, began swimming because Jack Wardrop had asthma. The family doctor wanted Jack to swim to build up his lungs. Twin brother Bert swam to keep Jack company. They became British champions, then came to college in the United States where Jack developed into the world's top swimmer with five world marks to his credit. Bert was not far behind, with one record in the tough four-stroke individual medley. Perhaps the only reason twin Jack was better than twin Bert, they both admit, is that Jack as a boy had the more serious purpose in becoming a swimmer. This serious purpose – the desire to win a battle with asthma or polio, the desire to swim your way to college education, or just to find something at which you can beat the boy down the street – is what motivates the thousands of competitive-minded youngsters in swimming.

In the fabulous Indianapolis Athletic Club team, 1958, 59, 60, 61, 62, 63, National AAU men's outdoor champions, were several examples of boys who had a real purpose in becoming champion swimmers. Frank McKinney, long time national backstroke champion and medal winner in two Olympics, is the son of a famous father, and Frank wanted to make his mark on his own. Swimming gave him his chance. George Breen, American 1,500 mtrs champion, and former world record-holder, had acne and was told to get out in the sun and to swim. Mike Troy, the national AAU 100 mtrs butterfly champion, lost his father when he was eight. No one on either side of his family had ever gone to college, but Dr Miles Barton, one of the Indianapolis Athletic Club's most ardent swimming fathers, convinced the boy he could use his talent to swim his way out of poverty. Mike got his college scholarship, swimming planted the idea of college, and created in Mike the desire to study and to get his education as well as the desire to be an Olympic champion.

'There are thousands of more subtle examples where swimming has helped people make adjustments to life,' says Peter Daland, coach of the Los Angeles Athletic Club and the University of Southern California, and of the 1964 U.S. Women's

Olympic team. 'The important thing,' he says, 'is to involve more children in competitive swimming, and that is where age-group does its job.'

It is above all a great exposure activity. 'Age-group uses the competitive instinct of kids to build up their interest in learning to swim well. The big boast,' says Daland, 'is that this programme and this programme alone brought 500,000 kids into swimming. No other programme in the AAU in any sport has done so much.'

Peter had two girls in the 1960 Olympic team, Carolyn House and Molly Botkin, both National champions, once age-group beginners. Molly Botkin, from Hollywood, began quite modestly in age-group as did House. I saw Molly win the 250 yard freestyle race in the Women's Nationals at West Palm Beach, and her coach told me how she came to be a national champion. 'When Molly was nine and a half, her mother took her around to the Sherman Oaks Swim Club for a summer activity,' he said. 'She was shy, backward, and inhibited, then, gradually, as she became prominent, she came out of her shell. You can't be a national champion in women's swimming and stay an Alice-sit-by-the-fire. By the time she was 16 Molly Botkin was a community leader and an open personality who initiated things. Her swimming ability is unique, but Molly's social emergence through the age-group programme is typical.'

Molly's father, Perry Botkin, is a prominent pluck-string instrument player. He is a show-business personality, a recording artist, accompanist for Bing Crosby, and he's been on the George Gobel show. Molly's two brothers, Ted and Bunny, are also talented, and they are older than she is. They are big, and handsome, and outgoing. Molly was just the kid sister, accepted, but shy and quiet, with no particular accomplishment to put her up on a level with her father and brothers. Mrs Virginia Botkin is the stabilizing influence in the family. She acted as a counter-balance for her husband and sons, but she was most concerned about Molly until Molly took to swimming, or until Mrs Botkin took Molly to swimming. She took Molly to every practice. At first, Molly wanted to swim, but not to work very hard at it. 'She's not a Spartan, but all girl and normal in her social instincts,' Peter Daland told me. 'She's big, but not a tomboy, and when she came to me she didn't like to work. She

93

would probably have dropped by the wayside when the distances got longer and the training got tough, but she had success in swimming from the start, success as in nothing else she had yet done. She simply got so good that she had a responsibility to carry on. Then she disciplined herself to work because she had the five Olympic circles in her eyes. She wanted to go to Rome, and she likes being a champion.'

Molly could not have done it alone, her coach believes. Her mother has been there with her all the time. 'She's the kind of balanced, sensible woman,' he says, 'that acts the way every kid would like her mother to be. Molly is not fenced in, but she's on solid ground, and knows where she stands. The mother will get there, too,' says Daland. 'She chaperones all our trips to the Nationals. I might be able to replace Molly, but the club could never get along without Mrs Botkin.'

At the Los Angeles Athletic Club, Molly was exposed to older children in a healthy atmosphere. She developed better work habits which raised her to a B plus student in school, as well as helped her swimming. The boys on the Los Angeles team were older, but they liked Molly, and admired her ability as a swimmer. There was no social barrier in the swimming pool, as there are class levels in school. When she was twelve and a half, in a team of 17- and 18-year-old girls, she missed being elected captain by just one vote. Molly was accepted and liked for herself. She knew what to talk about, and she learned to speak up, and she got along with older people. She learned that the swimming she was growing to love is a privilege, that the club had a rule that the swimmers' main responsibility is studying, and that they must drop out if the marks go down.

The real test came, when Molly was 16, in the Botkin dining-room at Sunday dinner. A guest had been questioning Perry Botkin and his boys on what they did. They told him about their music and he listened attentively. Then he asked Molly what she did. 'I swim,' she answered simply, and they all smiled.

'Molly's too modest,' said Perry Botkin. 'She's a national champion, and she's going to be on the Olympic team.' They all talked swimming the rest of the dinner hour, with Molly the centre of the conversation. The guest, who had been to Rome once before, said he wished he could swim, too.

'And what if she doesn't make it?' I asked her coach.

'She will,' said Peter, 'but the hard worker who doesn't win is still building a quality. Perhaps swimming isn't her line, but when she finds her ability field, that quality will pay off.'

Daland does not think age-group is perfect. He cites, as an example, Carolyn House, 1961 and 1962 high point winner of the outdoor nationals. At 12, House was fifth in the Women's National Senior 1,500-mtrs at Topeka, and she also scored eleven points in the Southern California Association Senior District Championships, yet in the 11–12 age-group she could not make the finals in any event in an eight lane pool. Carolyn, an outstanding prospect at the longer Olympic distances, just could not get going for the short races required in age-group rules. 'Limiting a contestant to short distances doesn't protect the swimmer's health,' he says. 'It retards his swimming development. A high school boy gets lazy. He doesn't have to train hard for 50's and 100's, and that is all he swims. When he gets to the longer distances required in college, or Olympic swimming, he may quit because he doesn't want to work so hard for the same glory he got by not working hard in high school and age-group.'

Beth Kaufman acknowledges this to be a problem, but she insists that the major purpose of age-group is to develop as many swimmers as possible. 'With shorter races we can have more races, and more swimming, in the same amount of time,' she says. 'With more kids competing, we'll help more learn to swim and it will be up to the coaches to develop the potential we turn up in age-group'

'Win or lose, our next Olympic swimming team will be awfully young,' Mrs Kaufman prophesied in 1958, 'perhaps the youngest and certainly the fastest we have ever had. It will come entirely out of age-group.' Carolyn House 14, and Donna de Verona 13, two California age-groupers, made Mrs Kaufman's prophesy come true. The oldest swimmers in the team were a ripe old 17 and these, too, were products of age-group swimming.

This is essentially the story of how age-group produced the U.S. girls' team that won the 1960 Olympics in Rome. The first products of age-group Ruuska, Kempner, Botkin and the incomparable Chris Von Saltza, were already 'old ladies' of 16 and 17. They were the first products of California age-group swimming. Becky Collins did not make the team but she came back in 1961. In 1964 (Tokyo) the U.S. boy's team as well as the girls were 100 per cent age-group alumni. Carolyn House did not repeat at 18, but Donna de Verona did at 17. The oldest girls who medaled were 18 (Cynthia Goyette and Sharon Finneran) but both had reached stardom since 1960. Youngsters were 14, not 13 as with Ruuska in 1956, and de Verona in 1960. Age-group was maturing, producing dozens of world class girls 14–18 and boys 16–22, the youngest Olympic sport for either sex because of the early start in age-group.

Age-group is the nearest thing to a nationally organized sports programme, and the biggest thing the United States and the Western world have produced in an Olympic sport. It brought competitive swimming to the forefront as a mass activity for our children. Now we must control and guide it in the U.S.A. to see that it stays healthy, and other countries must study it to see how such a programme might benefit their swimming.

Mrs Rose Mary Dawson and her husband, Buck Dawson, run Camp
Ak-O-Mak as a summer aquatic camp for age-group swimmers

Bumpy Jones, 1952 U.S. Olympic team and one-time world record holder Individual Medley. Jones began swimming at 10 at Matt Mann's camps and was still competing successfully at 30 when a practising M.D. He almost made the 1960 U.S. Olympic team on a comeback. All age-groupers don't quit. It is a matter of compatibility of interests

16

Why Your Daughter Should Swim

The following is an Open Letter which my husband and I sent to parents of all girls aged 8 to 18 in Ann Arbor. It explains why today's young girls and teenagers need an organized, competitive athletic programme, and solicits the parents' support in getting their daughters interested in such a programme. This letter could very well be used as a model by other organizations in other communities to persuade parents to help their children become active in age-group athletics.

Our first aim is to teach as many Ann Arbor girls as we can reach how to swim, or swim better, and ultimately how to swim well. Safety, and the pleasure of many water sports, demand that every child must swim.

Our second aim is to provide the only extra-mural competitive sports outlet for girls in Ann Arbor. We believe that our American way of life is competitive, that girls are competitive, and that a competitive sport is an ideal outlet for teenage tensions.

GIRLS MUST CONCENTRATE

We also believe that every child needs some one extra-curricular activity in which she must make a prolonged sustained effort to excel. With teenage girls, some physical outlet in sports is important to good health, beauty, physical fitness, and a balanced life. We believe in a balanced life, but we do not believe in developing a race of dilettantes. A girl must have the opportunity to excel in some one activity as well as the chance to try a smattering of all activities. Jumping from one thing to another, without paying the price in hard work to excel in one thing, is an American teenage tragedy most common in Ann Arbor, where many interests pull at every talented boy or girl. Examine your own adult life and see if self-discipline gained in a sport requiring hard work and dedication would have helped you learn to stick with it, to solve problems in your later life.

We believe in competition, and in some strenuous physical activity, and some consuming measured interest for every girl. We also believe swimming is a wonderful sport that is the best exercise there is. It is feminine, it builds beautiful bodies, it develops poise, and it saves lives.

Boys love 'varsity sports. Girls have no 'varsity sport except the Ann Arbor Swim Club. If you believe athletics are necessary for boys, then ask yourself why they are not just as important to girls. We believe they are, and we offer any Ann Arbor girl the experience of sport competition at all levels. We offer you the only local opportunity to have your girl participate in a competitive sport. This gives you a choice, and we believe the choice should be yours, and not ours, or the school principal's choice. We'll take any girl as far as she is willing and able to go, from beginner to Olympic champion, from inside the city limits, to halfway around the world.

None of this is easy, but do you want your daughter to have it easy? Why not give her a reason for not smoking, or drinking, in junior high and high school? Why not give her a group to belong to that stands for clean living and offers tangible rewards for clean living?

We will teach her how to accept victory and defeat through experience in a sports team. She will get recognition for her accomplishments, and make well-chaperoned trips, and meet fine people from other places. She will learn to make sacrifices and decisions. She will learn to plan her time and schedule herself – yes, she will become a better student in school because of swimming, and she will have something special to cling to when she is trying to find herself as a woman. She will belong to something – nothing superficial but something honest, measured on a stop-watch and counted in lengths of a pool. She cannot fool herself in swimming, and the lessons she learns in this competitive sport are measured in self-improvement. They carry over in life. So does the discipline.

GIRLS LEAD NORMAL LIVES

Does all this sound Spartan? It shouldn't. Most of the best swimmers lead very normal social lives. They are exceedingly popular, and usually quite social, but they are not over dependent on the vagaries of social life. They do not sit by the phone and wait, and they need make no compromises to be popular. They have two social lives: one in and through swimming, and one in and through their other local activities. Swimming takes them to meet champion boy swimmers from all over the country, giving them something in common with a superior group of young men, and out of town crushes that give them time to tend to business at home. Swimming is a topic of conversation, mutual understanding, respect, and it offers a very high moral code that binds amateur athletes in training for their sport. It also takes our swimmers to Canada, Florida, Puerto Rico, Jamaica, to live in the homes of fine people, and share in their experiences. At home, your daughter will be more selective in her social engagements, but not less popular, because of swimming.

Swimming requires some dedication, especially on the part of parents. If you believe in our programme you must be willing to sacrifice some convenience. Our better swimmers practise from 6.15 to 7.30 p.m. This means keeping meals hot in the oven, or otherwise adjusting your dinner routine to accommodate your daughter. It also means car pools, or perhaps driving alone four nights a week. Your child needs backing. This is not a school activity with school backing to help strengthen her determination to go on when it gets tough. This support must come from home. If the parents do not show an interest, it is much harder for the girl to work hard on her sport. She will not get backing from the crowd at the dime store. Most of our swimmers get their motivation from within, but there are always moments when the long-range dreams, and objectives of swimming practise are obscured by some momentary pleasure or outside pressure. This is where the girl swimmer wants her folks to say, 'Young lady, you signed up for this, now get going'.

We, the coach and manager, get discouraged, too, when a talented youngster quits. We can only hope she has quit for a good reason, and not to give herself more time for television, records, and the telephone. We are dedicated volunteers, even as the swimmers are. Their response is our reward, just as it will be yours, if you let it get to you. Few of us had the talent, or the guts, or the self-discipline, to become a state or national champion. When one of our children has this talent, we must back her (or him, for that matter) all the way. The teacher you remember is not the one who gave you a C for E work but the one who made you earn an A. We have a national obligation to standards of excellence in sports, too.

We will provide the incentive, you provide the support, and see what we can do to help the girls motivate themselves. We will let you know if your daughter's forte appears to be swimming; but even if it is not, she will have fewer colds (this we can prove statistically), feel, and look better, when she swims. We will do our best to be a good influence on her, too, and coaches have a particular advantage in this as they teach the activity that the child has chosen because she likes it.

If you believe in our programme, tell your friends, and support your daughter. Those two guys from Harvard disagreed on this. We are with the one who was in the White House, who wanted physical fitness, and not the one who talks to junior high principals about over-emphasis on sports. The idea of competitive sport for girls and children has been slow in gaining universal support with educators, but we would be glad to debate the benefits any time, and any place. We believe in what we are doing, and that helps, too.

17
Michigan's Development League—An Autumn Plan for Swimming

Age-Group Swimming does not answer all problems, nor do the mammoth age-group contests. Each area must also find a plan to bridge the gap between age-group and senior swimming, between novice and experience. Such a plan was, and is, our Michigan development league which my husband and I helped found a few years ago.

The Michigan Girls Swim League, as we call it, is a development programme during a time of the year when the club coaches are not quite so tied down with their winter and summer age-group and senior 'varsity programmes. The idea was initiated by Coach John Hussey of Wayne State University when he was coaching the Detroit Women's City Club several years ago. The league, currently, has teams from Toledo, Ohio, and Windsor, Ontario, plus five Michigan cities: Battle Creek, Grand Rapids, Flint, Ann Arbor, and Detroit. Each of these teams swims each other team in a dual contest schedule beginning the first of October and ending the middle of November. For newer clubs, the league team may also be the club 'varsity team while for the bigger and older clubs it is strictly a non-'varsity team to develop swimmers. Competition is kept even by a novice-type rule which prohibits any swimmer competing who has been placed first, second, or third, in a national or Association Senior or Junior Championship event. Relays, and age-group events, are not included in this disqualification clause. With the area's top swimmers ineligible, the league offers opportunity for everybody else to come into his own, regardless of age. There are late-developing high school seniors, and even college girls, swimming in the league, but the majority of competitors are 12-, 13-, 14-year-old swimmers eager to 'get a jump' on the winter age-group season and perhaps make the bigger jump to senior swimming which is stressed in the area.

Most of the area coaches have their 'varsity swimmers taking an early autumn lay-off, or a dry-land exercise programme, during this period, and this leaves the coaches free to devote in-the-water time to their fast developing 'novices.' The league encourages this development in several ways. Week-end dual contest competition is offered for seven consecutive weeks and under the most favourable conditions for improvement. Community backing is considerable since the league swimmers are not in competition with their peers, the AAU champions, who are between seasons. Here is an ideal opportunity for the coaches to develop that extra girl, or two, or three, they need to fill their 'varsity team which swings into action after the league season is over. Due to the slightly lower level of controlled competition, these swimmers are never discouraged by the big jump to 'varsity and they often improve so rapidly that the jump is small or non-existent, by the time the league has its championship contest around Thanksgiving.

Hussey had another motive when he started the league. In Michigan, as elsewhere, there are a great many summer country club teams and relatively much fewer winter AAU clubs offering swimming. The country club sprinters are used to short distances, and lots of publicity. The new swimming league is designed to catch these girls before they have lost interest and conditioning. The league offers them a transition to longer, and more difficult, AAU races. The dual contests offer a compact two-hour contest with 50's and 100's in each stroke plus 200 yds relays, low board diving, 100 Individual Medley, and 200 yds Freestyle, a total of thirteen events. Covering these events forces a coach to give more swimmers a chance since league rules limit each swimmer to three events, one of which must be a relay. By dual contest rules, a team needs two swimmers to cover each event, and in six lane pools extra competitors are encouraged to use the extra lanes. This also applies to relays where B and C relays swim exhibition.

There are several factors which lend glamour to the league, and offer the swimmers encouragement through recognition by press and public. Membership qualifications for the league lend themselves to inter-city rivalry since no one club can stay on top with its older swimmers, most of whom will disqualify themselves by medalling in their association championships. This makes the league title race a seesaw affair from year to year. It also means that natural geographic rivalries between nearby communities can be exploited during a season when the local sports editors are starved for news other than football. The league offers a trophy to the team with the best won-lost record, and weekly changes in the standings, race results, and anticipation of upcoming contests means at least one, and usually two, stories a week. A league all-star team is picked from best times turned in during the dual racing season, and a championship meeting and trophy at the end of the season offer everybody a second chance. League records are kept for both dual and championship meets, with all-star and championship medals as individual incentives. The dual and championship team trophies are also frequently split with two teams dividing honours as league champions. There are no expensive travel costs and no entry fees other than a $22.00 season fee per team, which covers the expense of the various trophies and medals. There is the added attraction that all Ann Arbor home contests are held in the new University Women's Pool on Saturday mornings with the visiting team guests at a Michigan football game in the afternoon. The Championship meet is a gala all-day affair at the new Flint Junior College Durham Natatorium. There are no limits on the number of entries per event in the Championship races.

Michigan age-group meets are planned to end the last weekend in November, or early in December, as are the Toledo Glass City Relays, and Battle Creek Cereal Bowl Relays. This offers incentive for the younger league swimmers to go right on after the league championships. The league provides interest, sustaining continuity for all 'eager beaver' youngsters who would want no part of a fall lay-off. 'Old pros' who do like a lay-off help officiate the races, or play week-end water polo during this season. The league does not create a false sense of values, as summer country club swimming sometimes does, because the 'varsity swimmers and the coach are around to remind them of bigger goals to come. Big clubs like the Glass City Aquatic Club of Toledo, and the Ann Arbor Swim Club, find the league fills a void, and encourages development of swimmers who might be overlooked by the age and skill qualification of age-group and senior AAU swimming contests.

103

I have had swimmers begin in this league and go on to become national finalists, and champions in senior swimming and water polo. I considered it part of a complete programme in Ann Arbor, which also included teaching classes, age-group and senior swimming. Because of the lower skill level to begin with, the progress of the league swimmers is rapid and exciting. It is the difference between high school and college coaching in men's swimming. In high school, the coach must start from scratch and do what he can to put a team in the water and meet his schedule commitments. You lose your swimmer on graduation, and there is no recruiting. Every coach has a chance.

The Michigan Swimming League is for girls only, largely because there is no girls' programme in Michigan high schools. The league fills a need in girls club swimming in Michigan but there is no reason why any area cannot form a similar autumn development league for boys, girls, or both. In Michigan, at least, it has proved a big success. All but one of last year's Michigan Girls AAU Swim Champions were graduates of the league. Michigan swimming has definitely benefited from the league in more new clubs, and better swimming in the old clubs. Perhaps an autumn development league can fill a slack season and help build up more swimming for more people in your area, too.

Swimmers from U.S., Canada, Mexico and Puerto Rico meet in Fort Lauderdale, Florida, for two weeks' training with Mrs Dawson at College Coaches (Christmas Vacation) Swim Forum

Florida Christmas reunions are one way Mrs Dawson keeps swimmers interested in off-season. The three small children to left of Matt Mann (centre) are his age-group swimming grandchildren. Mr Buck Dawson is on the extreme right

Age-group swimmers waiting for their Saturday morning races at Ryde in Sydney, Australia, where Forbes Carlile is the professional coach

Young age-group swimmers at Camp Ab-O-Mak, Ann Arbor

18

One Other Way to Keep Our Children from Quitting

'Senior-itis' has always been a problem in college boys swimming. Some of the boys are sick of training and ready to quit before graduation. It is an occupational hazard of any amateur sport that demands long hours of hard and perhaps monotonous work. No sport is more time-consuming than swimming in this type of methodical training. This lack of desire is unfortunate timing in an almost-graduated college senior. This is much more of a tragedy for a boy or girl who is fed up even before he or she starts high school.

After years of search for what is mostly good and a bit that is bad about age-group swimming, I have come to the conclusion that the big drop-out rate in the early teens is perhaps the worst feature. There are many social factors of course, but this problem is partly due to the nature of age-group meets and this can be corrected. Most age-group swimming meets have 3 or 4 events in each age group, making it possible for one girl (or boy) to dominate her age group. While a boy or girl is moving to the top, a better time or a 6th place ribbon or filling in on a relay is ample reward, but once on top, most swimmers must stay on top to stay interested. This means that one team-mate improving more rapidly or even one swimmer from another team who is improving more rapidly can overtake the current champion who then becomes the ex-champion and rapidly loses face and interest even though this ex-champion's times may still be improving. Zealous mothers and other swimmers happy to see the ex-champion get her come-up-once ask leading questions such as, 'What's wrong with Kathy lately?' or 'Isn't it a shame that Connie has been beating your Kathy?' and the ex-champion and her Mom pack their bags and leave the circuit.

Just the change from the top of one age-group to the bottom

of another causes many such drop-outs, for face-saving reasons alone, parent face-saving as often as offspring. The ultimate Olympic champion survives but the scrap pile is much larger than necessary. If there were more team swimming with dual meets where a 2nd or 3rd place point can be all-important to team victory, this situation would not come up. There will always be a need for omnibus age-group meets and championships but there must be more dual meets where a coach must have a dozen or more swimmers *and divers* to cover his events. With restriction on the number of events (2 or 3) per swimmer, no single star can win a dual meet. There must be a team, and team victory becomes more important than any one star performance, team points are more important than times. There is pressure on the also-rans not to quit because the team needs the points, rather than pressure on them to quit while ahead. National Age-Group best times and large age-group meets cater to the *current* star and the rising aspirant but dual meets are needed to keep children in swimming longer, to give them a team spirit, and to accommodate the late bloomer who may come on strong in the late teens.

Every season must be a blend of both types of meets. American boys get this blend in high school and college swimming. Girls and boys must also have it as an incentive to stay in age-group swimming – to keep them off the scrap heap, which among other things, heaps criticism on our whole competitive programme by our critics among anti-competitive recreation and physical education people who don't want swimming races at any high level. Even with those who are completely sold on the competitive Olympic dream, it must be acknowledged that many children quit too soon to know if they might have made it. Any step to help our age-group programme keep more children from quitting will help swimming. A 'true athlete', that is a matured, adult, true athlete with unconditional commitment, may not be able to quit but our problem in age-group is not the adult swimmer but how to keep the near-adult in swimming.

19

Towards a Better Philosophy in American Women's Physical Education

As we discussed in earlier chapters, Age-Group can not do the whole job of Olympic development, or even of limited early exposure in all sports without endorsement by the educators. In any country where youth sports are organized and controlled primarily through the schools, there must be institutional backing if a majority of our most talented children are to participate.

The weakest link in the United States sports exposure, and probably in most other countries, is in women's sports. This chapter is an appeal to my colleagues in women's physical education for changes in attitude which I believe are necessary before we will get adequate sports, or even adequate fitness, in our girls, and all children taught by women physical education teachers. This appeal is important to parents of highly motivated and skilled children because it outlines some of the problems you must face in getting adequate school programmes for your children.

The present pre-occupation with youth physical fitness gives us a golden opportunity to raise the status of our profession by doing a better job in women's physical education. To do this, it may be necessary to re-evaluate our whole philosophy of women's physical education, and see how we can make our profession more compatible with public interest as well as public need. In a democracy such as ours, public opinion is even more important than the status we attain with professional colleagues. School-boards still retain control of the educational purse strings. We cannot get more money, and more facilities for more women's physical education teachers, unless we can present a programme more compatible with public interest. Our greatest allies in getting more and better physical education are more likely to be the fitness-conscious parents; the tax-payers and the government than the school principal, the superintendent and our faculty colleagues pre-occupied with keeping a larger percentage of the education dollar for academic pursuits.

We are underrating the importance of our profession if we accept a rung at the bottom of the academic ladder. The old cliché, 'school-work must come first!' is a standard American truism, but so is the philosophy that, 'a man hasn't got anything if he hasn't got his health!' You cannot walk into a hospital and convince anyone there that good maths and good English are more important than good health. You would expect an English teacher, or an academic-oriented school official, to believe that maths, English, and history, must come first, but it is ridiculous when physical education teachers subscribe to this view. If we are to have equal status in the academic community, we must define 'school-work must come first' to include physical education. 'Book-work must come first' is not school-work must come first, and book-work without companion physical activity is a travesty on the term physical education.

It seems ridiculous in a country crying for better physical fitness, that physical educators would docilely accept the idea that English shall be compulsory throughout high school and college, yet compulsory physical education often ends in junior high school. Even when gym is compulsory, we arbitrarily settle for two or three times a week, yet every physical educator knows that less than one hour a day is insufficient for even a sub-standard level of fitness. It is time we quit excusing this situation by the shortage of women physical education teachers and find a way to create conditions which will demand more women physical education teachers. We cannot defer to extra-curricular sports and then damn extra-curricular sports. We cannot damn competition, if our competitive society will become more interested in fitness programmes when they are competitive programmes. We must stop preaching the abuses of coaches, and train our own people to coach. We cannot write off the specially skilled and call ourselves competent teachers. Until we can train our own coaches, we must abandon the concept that men coaches should not be allowed to coach women. Until they are allowed to coach our women majors, we will not have women to coach. We will never be accepted as teaching equals so long as we insist on segregation from the men. Why should we isolate ourselves? How can we improve our situation with such an ingrown attitude? Women English teachers teach boys, and men teach girls. Our obsession against the nickname 'Phys. Eds.' is a self-conscious confession of our inferiority. What difference does it make what they call us? For years, students have gone to 'Engine School'. Why not 'Phys. Ed.' class?

We must earn the respect by performance, and stop trying to achieve it by rank and title. Only we can lead the way and stop the nonsense that hard exercise is bad for girls, that girls should sit out their menstrual cycle, and be excused from gym, that men cannot teach girls because they don't understand these things, that girls are more emotionally disturbed by competition. There may be isolated examples of such things, but we cannot downgrade our whole programme because of them. There are also two-hundred-pound girls who should not drink milk, but we do not condemn milk drinking for girls. The practice which is bad, bad for health, comfort, and parent-teacher relations, is giving fitness tests without any previous buildup in conditioning. No coach worthy of that title would ask his athletes for a maximum effort with no buildup training programme. Yet, we physical education teachers do this all too frequently and send the children home so stiff and sore that they can barely walk.

In a society and school system where everyone competes, we must also compete, and use the popularity of competition to advance our programmes. Accelerated classes, debating, the school orchestra, spelling bees – all of these things are competitive. Why not physical education? We extol the evils of extramural activity and strike the word 'Varsity from our vocabulary, yet we find ourselves in the position where students who love to compete elsewhere in school hate gym because the challenge is too vague. We need to make gym compulsory every day, for good health reasons, but we will not get this concession until we concede that competitive games can make our activity popular. Exercise has always been more popular as part of a game, and games are competitive. Intramurals have never been as popular with Americans as 'Varsity because Americans dream of being the biggest and best. We cannot change the American, so let's use it. The most popular and successful physical education programmes have been in the small schools, where everyone has a chance to make 'Varsity in something. We need many more 'varsity teams, so that more children are included, rather than

109

no 'varsity teams so that no one is left out. Intramurals are most popular in schools that have a 'Varsity tradition for which the intramural and gym class student aspires and perspires. We must change from a negative to a positive philosophy. We must train ourselves, and our best students, to step in and coach rather than stand back and condemn coaches. To cure coaching abuses, we must join and reform rather than criticize without a popular counter-programme. We must appeal to our specially talented and not downgrade everything to the lowest common denominator.

We must change our attitude towards specialists who want to enter our field. At Michigan, I had the idea that we were motivated by fear. Because most of us lacked the qualifications to handle a specially-skilled major, we tended to condemn the specially skilled. We took the attitude that a champion girl athlete coming into our department as a freshman was a dangerous intruder. We convinced ourselves that an all-round major could not be a specialist in any one field without her perspective being warped out of proportion. We took the attitude that no specialist could be trained for all-round physical education teaching skills. I believe we limit ourselves by this attitude, driving most of our outstanding women physical education prospects into other fields. The drop out at Michigan is enormous.

The men in physical education recognize many athletic abuses, but they have gained bigger budgets, better facilities, better jobs, and better status for all of us because of parent and student interest in competitive sports. Many outstanding men physical educators began as coaches and *vice versa*. Often the two fields combine to provide necessary salaries to keep good men in the field.

The abuses are mostly in the big money sports, football, and basketball. Even these can be controlled. Minor sport coaches are never fired for losing. Women do not need to accept the abuses of athletic scholarships, and they will not lose their jobs if they put their record on the line in minor competitive sports. At Michigan, we told our majors that coaching aborts many good physical education teachers. This is sometimes true, but just as often it works in reverse. In our area, many young men who began as 'varsity athletes and coaches have withdrawn from the coaching profession, at or near the top, to concentrate on the enormous challenges in physical education. Olympic swimmer and swim coach, Dr William Heusner, Canadian Olympic swim coach, Dr John Faulkner, former 'Varsity swim coaches, Dr T. K. Cureton and Dr Earle Zeigler, were head coaches who left coaching jobs to assume greater roles in other areas of physical education. These teachers would certainly never condemn 'Varsity athletics, and athletic specialists, as undesirables in physical education. The energy, enthusiasm, and discipline, generated first in competitive sports has carried over into their physical education work. What has been for these men can also apply for women. Ann Ross is a wonderful example. We can use the men as a guide, profit by their mistakes as well as their positive experience, but let's stop ignoring our common interests and isolating our women. In the public view, coaching and physical education teaching are synonymous. We must stop spending so much time fighting the public view.

With the challenge, and the opportunity offered right now, we must seize on this chance to raise our status and increase our influence, and numbers, in a great, big, needed way. It is time we quit defending our small sanctuary and go on the offensive towards the big big world that is our future.

There has been an alarming under-emphasis on physical fitness in our society *and our schools* that shows up in draft board physicals, and in the general fitness of our youth compared with the countries we consider our competitors. If we are to change our way of life to include a healthy proportion of physical exercise, we must begin in our schools. Our pre-teens are active. After that, we must replace this loss of unselfconscious physical activity with organized exercise. The twelve and teens are where the breakdown begins, and this is where we should increase our influence to provide more and better physical education. It will be popular if we make it popular with the stimulus of high standards, regular activity, games, competitive urge, energy, and imagination. We must do a job, create a better programme and then sell it so that women's physical education can come into its own as a key part of every curriculum. Only in this way can we increase our numbers, and our influence, incidentally getting better pay, more respect, and the satisfaction of an important job well done.

20

Bringing Up Father

by Carlos Sala

*Carlos Sala is a native Puerto Rican who has been coaching
five years with great success. I had the pleasure of getting to
know him on two separate occasions when I went to Puerto
Rico to help train swimmers for international competition. His
team, the Condado Beach Hotel Porpoise Club of San Juan,
won the Puerto Rico senior island championships two years in
a row, and Sala has developed many of the island's outstanding
senior swimmers through age-group growing pains. He coached
the 1961 and 1963 Central American age-group teams, and
the senior Central American Games team in 1962.*

*Sala is a member of the American Swimming Coaches Asso-
ciation and he has spent a great deal of time in Florida at clinics,
observing the workings of American Age-Group Swimming.
Puerto Rico, unlike most American Association areas, goes to
great expense to send age-group teams to international competitions. Whether this helps or hurts senior competition remains to be seen as Puerto Rican Senior Swimming (since age-
group) is just now coming of age.*

*Here is Sala's philosophy for Age-Group as it applies to
Puerto Rico and perhaps in your country, as well.*

SWIMMING, like school, like the Boy Scouts, or like the many
varied activities that our children invariably become involved in, is an integral part of home life. Swimming is truly
part of the process of growing up; it is not so much a final gold
medal, or a performance that is designed to gladden the heart
of the doting parent, it is rather a means whereby much that
is to be learned is learned. For Junior must learn to fight
through many many laps of practice, he must learn how to
live with his team mates, he must learn that before he is good,
he must be bad, and before he is to win he must lose. On the

mental plane, he must learn to evaluate his abilities, supplement his weaknesses, and make good use of his strength and his developed abilities. The parents enter into this process and could either help and encourage, or frustrate and discourage. The parents are very much the key to the child's future in the Sport, and, with the proper understanding, much can be done just as truly as much can be ruined by improper understanding and compulsive behaviour.

Over-anxious parents can do a great deal of harm, and perhaps even permanent harm to the child. The swimmer in competition is already under considerable stress. The additional stress imposed by the parents for the child to win can well be overdone. Parents must not lose sight of the fact that the real benefit to the child comes from working up to the winning point, rather than necessarily winning; he must not be driven to win before he is able to win, otherwise his incentive is lost and no amount of parental pressure can restore the true incentive. Over-anxious parents tend to drive their children to win for their own satisfaction rather than for the benefit to the child. The child will then fear a bad performance and the subsequent punishment, physical or mental, from the parent. Thus can begin constant nagging, belittling of the child. The swimmer becomes nervous, performance decays, and a vicious cycle sets in, the worse the performance, the more the abuse.

I have seen situations arise in which the relationship got to a point at which the parent threatened to withdraw a child from a sport he truly enjoyed. One result was that the child became discourteous to the parents and, naturally, matters became worse and eventually the child gave up the sport. The irony is often that the child would have done well and would have gained much benefit and confidence from continuing.

Parental problems generally do not start until the child has achieved some small success in a race. The moment a child places well, parents become difficult. They become involved in a sport which generally they know nothing about. They ask for *ridiculous* and impossible drops in time; if the child should be a breaststroker, the parent immediately becomes a breaststroke expert. Some parents get the feeling that if it were not for their necessity for making a living, they would be the best coach for their child. These parents who go to such extents are never satisfied with the coach and tend to change coaches; in truth, they believe that no coach but they themselves can do justice to Junior. Poor Junior, in the meantime, is just trying to keep up with his team, do his best in competition, and learn to get along with the high pressure world around him.

It is disheartening for a coach to see his swimmer fall apart because his parents have no idea what it is all about. Fortunately, most parents do not get to extreme points with their children, and one way or the other the children and the parents and the team end up benefitting by the relationship. I know it is difficult for parents to control themselves when they gain so much interest in Junior's progress. However, it is also difficult for the coaches to maintain the happy balance that will give Junior his best chance of success in the sport.

From the team and team activities, Junior will learn much that will carry over into adulthood. He will learn companionship, team spirit, physical fitness, loyalty, working habits, determination, acceptance of defeats as well as victories, and he will learn self-evaluation. The road is certainly tough, and full of pitfalls. Parents must know when to encourage, when to give that pat on the back, just as well as he must know when a little toughness is called for. Likewise, there are pitfalls for the parents, and I am sure that the best of them will sometimes fall in and Junior will temporarily give up. However, this is all part of growing up and when there is basic understanding of what Junior is up against, every downward trend will be followed by that much improvement.

21

Age-Group Swimming in Britain

by W. J. Juba

(Assistant Editor of the *Swimming Times*)

THERE is almost certain to be a national Age-Group Championship in England in 1966.

Following Britain's disappointing swimming performances at the 18th Olympic Games in Tokyo, in October 1964, officials who had been pressing hard for the setting up of a national age-group scheme for a number of years look like winning through. A committee was formed in late 1964 to discuss organisation and submit recommendations to the Amateur Swimming Association on the possibility of a national competition.

I understand that an English business firm has offered to sponsor such a competition for three years to the extent of covering the considerable out-of-pocket expenses involved. In addition, they would be prepared to provide a sum of £500 per annum for an official to organise the competitions

It was suggested that the age-groups should be nine to ten years of age; ten to eleven years; eleven to twelve years; twelve to thirteen years and thirteen to fourteen years.

The proposed events are backstroke, breaststroke, butterfly and front crawl. Plus an individual medley for the twelve years and over.

It was also recommended that there should be three entrants for each event from each of the geographic districts in England of the Amateur Swimming Association. Swimmers would be restricted to competing in three events only.

Mr Alfred Price, the 1964 British Olympic team manager, who has been advocating national age-group swimming in Britain for years, commented in his official Olympic report at the conclusion of the Tokyo Games that the reason for the American domination of world swimming is the terrific amount of competition in which they are engaged. In the first instance this is secured through age-group swimming competitions held throughout the American continent.

Age-Group Swimming is nothing new in England. It has taken place in various forms at local levels since the conclusion of the last world war. Although it has been organised rather haphazardly with no real national pattern. In fact, the author's father, the late Matt Mann, who left Leeds to become one of the United States most celebrated Olympic swimming coaches, was an age-group swimmer in England before 1900!

About ten years ago a form of age-group competition involving hundreds of children took place in London. This comprised a number of talent spotting contests organised by the Southern Counties Amateur Swimming Association. The competitors raced in various age ranges, strokes and distances. They were timed and a well-known coach was allocated to each lane to comment to a shorthand writer on the participants stroke and potential. Enthusiasm for this meeting was so terrific that I would have thought at that time a national scheme would have been considered.

The celebrated Judy Grinham, winner of the women's 100 m. backstroke at the 1956 Olympic Games in Melbourne, European and British Commonwealth champion plus 100 m. and 110 yds backstroke world record-holder, was discovered at one of these contests.

Another popular form of age-group contests held nation wide is the English Schools' Championships organised by the English Schools' Amateur Swimming Association. Many national champions and international stars have emerged from the ranks of these championships.

Early in the season thousands of schoolchildren start the trail towards an ultimate national schools title through city, town, and area meetings. From these contests the representatives to compete in the national championships are chosen.

Some idea of the national schools' standard can be gained from the following winners times :

Boys: 13 to 16 years : 110 yds freestyle, A. Berman, 59.9; 110 yds backstroke, J. Rogers, 1 :07.8; 110 yds breaststroke, R. Roberts, 1 :16.1; 110 yds butterfly, I. Johnson, 1 :05.1; $293\frac{1}{3}$ yds individual medley, A. Kimber, 3 :31.9.

Girls: 13 to 16 years: 110 yds freestyle, P. Sillett, 1 :06.2; 110 yds backstroke, J. Franklin, 1 :13.4; 110 yds backstroke, S. Churms, 1 :22.2; 110 yds butterfly, A. Brindley, 1 :17.1; 293⅓ yds individual medley, L. Cole, 3 :54.5.

Boys: 16 to 19 years: 110 yds freestyle, D. Watts, 58.6; 110 yds backstroke, P. Burke, 1 :05.7; 110 yds breaststroke, M. Tucker, 1 :14.9; 110 yds butterfly, M. Turner, 1 :03.7; 293⅓ yds individual medley, J. Matthissen, 3 :26.6.

Girls: 16 to 19 years: 110 yds freestyle, S. Keen, 1 :05.9; 110 yds backstroke, R. Hoare, 1 :13.3; 110 yds breaststroke, D. Harris, 1 :20.6; 110 yds butterfly, A. Cotterill, 1 :13.2; 293⅓ yds individual medley, G. Foy, 3 :50.0.

Scottish and Welsh Schools' Swimming Associations operate similar schemes.

A well-known British amateur coach and official, Mr Dickie Brown, of Hull, has been the prime mover in the effort to put national age-group swimming on a correct footing in this country.

In an endeavour to ascertain whether it would be in the interest of the sport for age-group swimming to be developed nationally, hundreds of questionaires and circulars were despatched to clubs in 1962. From the replies the Amateur Swimming Association was able to construct a comprehensive background as to the value of age-group swimming in England. One example of the interest shown in this type of competition was seen in 1964, when the Kent County Amateur Swimming Association held three age-group meetings at which about six hundred entrants competed at each. Sixty officials were required to control the 125 races.

Another typical example is the Southern Counties junior inter-county competition in which 500 selected swimmers from the various counties comprising the South of England compete annually. Ages ranged progressively from under ten years to sixteen years.

Even diving could go Age-Group in Great Britain. In an effort to provide a reservoir of young divers necessary to sustain an adequate flow of material to senior levels, Britain's diving administrators have discussed the practicability of introducing age-group diving.

Swimming demands dedicated hard work and youngsters who have not yet made the grade in national championships will find a competitive outlet in age-group competition, instead of just cracking away at the rather monotonous grind of training.

The healthy rivalry that should develop and the added interest should provide the incentive for harder training. This in turn would lead to a general all-round improvement in times.

There is no doubt that introduction of Age-Group Swimming could affect the future of thousands of what would remain unknown young swimmers in Britain.

Age-Group Swimming in Australia and Holland

by Forbes Carlile, M.Sc.

(Former Australian and Dutch National and Olympic Coach)

'As the young twig is bent, so it will grow.' This is surely the philosophical basis for age-group swimming. It is true physiologically – it is true psychologically. The whole development and adaptation of the young organism in a certain direction depends on the early use to which the organism is put. You cannot start training a musician or an acrobat at 13 or 14 years of age. Nor can you start teaching and training a swimmer at this age and expect him to hold his own in today's swimming world.

That the youngster must start training and competing early if success in swimming is the goal, is now widely accepted in the U.S.A. and in Australia. But old ideas and old prejudices 'die hard'. One must coach and try to influence swimming people in the 'old world', as we tried for 3 years to do in Holland, to know that instituting age-group swimming and competition is much easier *said* than done in countries with old traditions in medicine and physical education.

During our association with Dutch swimming as National coach from 1962 to 1964 it amazed us to hear in the Netherlands, doctors of the swimming Medical Committee raising every conceivable objection to the introduction of an age-group system as seen in the U.S.A.

It horrified them to think of under 14-year-old boys or girls racing at 400 mtrs and even by 1964 we had not been successful in having such an event included in any swimming programme. It was not permitted for clubs to have races for under 10's at more than 25 mtrs or for under 12's to race more than

119

50 mtrs. It was considered by the medical advisers of the Dutch Swimming Association to be almost criminal to race 12-year-old swimmers at 100 mtrs butterfly-stroke. It was considered to be detrimental to the child's health to allow him to race or train as hard as young Australians or Americans. These ideas were by no means confined to Holland. They were prevalent throughout the European countries, in France, Italy, Germany and to some extent Great Britain.

When I told the Dutch Medical Committee that in more than 20 years experience in training young swimmers I had never seen any evidence of the harmful effects of such training, and that evidently the American doctors could see no objection either, they shook their heads knowingly and told me that 'really it was to the more knowledgeable *German* doctors they turned for guidance and advice in these matters'.

I had a trump card in the form of evidence from one of the world's foremost authorities in sport medicine, Professor Ernst Jokl, M.D. Dr Jokl was formerly a *German* and a famous physician-scientist. Now he teaches and carries out research at the University of Kentucky, U.S.A. When Dr Jokl came to Holland lecturing at a symposium on Nutrition in 1962 I thought the opportunity was too good to miss for confronting members of the Dutch Medical Committee with some first-hand evidence favouring extensive age-group swimming.

The Dutch doctors asked Professor Jokl how much training an 11- or 12-year-old could do. The Professor made this reply: 'They can do all that a coach like Carlile might ask, even 6 miles a day of interval training. Gentlemen I believe you are frightened of an "Abominable Snowman" – something which *does not exist*. There is NO medical evidence to suggest that the young growing organism cannot be exposed without harm to very hard training.'

However there are still in Holland strict rules controlling competition for 8-, 9- and 10-year-olds. Parents, understandably, share the fears of the doctors when it comes to both racing and training.

In 1964 progress was made in Holland when age races down to under 12 years (50 mtrs for this age) were included at the

Age-group swimmers from New England (Boston area) training at
Rose Mary Dawson's Canadian camp

This trio won National AAU medley relay title for Matt Mann
(background) in years prior to U.S. Age-Group programme. Boy on
left is Matt Mann, Jr., now coaching High School swimming in
Lansing, Michigan. Mann's camp was an age-group forerunner to
the present programme

A coach often doesn't know whether she is coming or going. Mrs
Dawson's routine, beside keeping house, is to coach a University
women's swim team, a senior club team, age-group team, novice team,
swim classes, diving classes and to run the swim programme at her
summer camp. Here she packs in her Ann Arbor bedroom between
trips to Puerto Rico and Japan. Her question, like any other woman's,
'What to wear?'

National Championships in August. Similar moves are being taken in many European countries and International Age-Group Meets for under 16-year-old swimmers are now held annually.

After the stimulus that the great American successes in Tokyo has given, we are sure to see a gradual expansion in age-group competition in Europe. But, could an American or an Australian believe this fact? There is no school or inter-school swimming competition in most European countries and none at all in Holland. Nor is there any move to introduce school competition.

It will take a long time to 'get through' and change opinions of educationalists in Europe. Even physical education leaders are very guarded in expressing opinions on the benefits of age-group competition.

I have heard two main objections from educationalists in Europe. Firstly, success in swimming is said to be 'psychologically' bad for the young boy and girl. Secondly, swimming training and competition is considered to be in direct opposition to academic education. Swimmers find themselves thwarted at school in most athletic ambitions. Quite a few Dutch head-masters have said to enthusiastic swimmers – 'Take your pick, your education or your sport' – as though education only involved class rooms and study.

One day we shall have a scientific study on the academic status of our competitive swimmers at Ryde in Sydney. For six months of the year our large team, like others all over Australia is at the pool at 6 a.m. for training and again in the afternoon at 4 p.m. for another strenuous session. We are certain that swimmers who learn to organise their lives to train regularly and hard, despite the time it takes, are on the average *better* at their school work than those who live what some call a 'normal existence'. We find that many of our pupils besides being at the top of their classes at school have wide and varied interests. They are well-rounded individuals who are community-minded and able to do much more than swim.

I recall that Australian David Theile, twice Olympic backstroke champion (1956 and 1960) was a brilliant medical student and always in the top three in his year. Another of our former age-group pupils David Hawkins, Olympic butterfly swimmer in 1952, is now an Assistant Professor at Harvard. The life-story of many of Australia's great swimmers like Sir Frank Beaurepaire, and Billy Longworth is a success story as I am sure will be the story of the great American champion Don Schollander, always an outstanding age-grouper and a 'straight A' student at High School, now at Yale University. He is one of hundreds, perhaps thousands who have shown that competitive swimming at a very high level, *and* a successful social and academic life do MIX WELL.

Time and time again school teachers and headmasters tell us of difficult and lazy pupils who have taken up hard training in one of our or other coach's groups and soon have improved at school in every way. The discipline of training has a carry-over effect.

I mentioned that another objection levelled at the participation of young children in swimming competition by European educationalists is that it is claimed to be psychologically bad for a young boy or girl to be successful and to *win*. We found that many of the Dutch opponents to a full age-group programme, not being able to present evidence of medical ill effects of training, fell back on the less tangible 'psychological' reason to justify their objections. In all seriousness it was pointed out to us more than once that 'intensive age-group training and competition could only go on in countries like the U.S.A. and Australia WHERE THEY DO NOT LOOK AFTER THEIR CHILDREN'.

Perhaps I am being hard on my European friends. However I believe that it is important to bring into the open the untenable objections which have been allowed for so long to hold back the proper advancement of swimming in most of Europe. Even now I know that in Holland young swimmers are not given nearly the same opportunity to succeed in competitive swimming as in the U.S.A. and, to a lesser extent, in Australia. To put it frankly, the officials of many countries are in my view, hidebound by old traditions which are holding up the progress of competitive swimming.

It would be incorrect to say that 'nothing' was happening in age-group swimming in Holland and other European countries. Practically all have now introduced more age-group championships and, as I have mentioned some, including France, Great Britain and West Germany held International Age-Group Meets in 1964 and more are planned for the future. Sweden has for a number of years pushed forward with fairly extensive age-group competitions and has a good National programme for training youngsters, but Holland, France and Italy have been very slow in developing their youth at competitive swimming.

There are a handful of very fine swimmers in Europe, but in depth the Europeans are far behind the U.S.A. This is in spite of combined Europe having a total population even in excess of America's. Of course, lack of swimming facilities is a great problem in many countries but even in the pools they do have, it is my impression that European officials must press on faster with their plans and quickly reach more young people with good modern training. The 'writing has been on the wall' for some time now. It must be read, understood and acted upon or Europe will continue to be the 'poor relation' in the world of swimming.

Australia won 4 swimming gold medals at Tokyo, which, apart from Russia's one gold medal were the only first places not captured by the great all-round U.S.A. team composed almost entirely of ex-age-groupers.

How has Australia, despite a population of only 11 million been able to keep up even to the extent it has, with the tremendous American advances since 1956? The answer is development of AGE-GROUP swimming.

Before 1956 when Australian swimmers amazed and alarmed the Americans by winning 8 gold medals, Australia had more age-group training and competition. But then the shocked reaction of coaches and officials in the U.S.A. resulted in the great system of youth participation in swimming that we see today.

A counter-reaction did not get under way in Australia until about 1962. It took a long time for swimming officials to absorb the hard fact that we were being beaten at our own game. Australian officials had, since 1956 basked in the reflected glory of a few outstanding competitors. They could, or would not see that the depth was not there and Australian top competitors were falling in world standing.

However, after the Rome Olympics when Australia had demonstratably slipped well behind the U.S.A., once again there started in Australia a move to extend age-group competition.

Briefly this is the present situation in Australia which, although not perfect is a move in the right direction.

Swimming clubs usually conduct handicap races for boys and girls of all ages (Even at 4 years of age!) every week-end from October when the outdoor pools open, until the end of March. Practically all swimming is in outdoor 50 m. pools. In November and December there are Inter-club competitions but the great weakness is that the best swimmers do not get adequate racing experience. Top swimmers of all ages do not get more than one or two serious races until early January, when State Championships are held, followed by the National Under 16 years Championships in early February and Open Championships in early March. Like N.S.W. the strongest swimming State, most of the other 5 States of Australia have now separated into various Meets the age-group championships, from under 10 years to under 14. In N.S.W. these are held in mid-February. Because of the travelling involved in a country nearly the same as the U.S.A. (but with 1/17 the population), no *National* Championships are held for swimmers under the age of 14 years.

In addition to the Club, State and National races mentioned above the various States nearly all hold what are known as 'TOP-TEN' Trials. These are at all strokes from under 10 years to open. Two distances are raced over 100 mtrs and 200 mtrs (yes even 200 mtrs butterfly under 10 years!).

Together with school and inter-school championships in March, this represents the competitive season for an Australian swimmer. The age-grouper gets more competition than the older swimmer for whom the Australian Swimming Union and its State Associations have very little to offer. This is one of the big complaints of the swimmers and the professional coaches who train 90 per cent of the serious competitive swimmers in Australia – there is not enough first class competition. Even so, the position in Australia is very much more 'healthy' in regard to racing and in youth training than in Europe generally.

In age-group organsiation it is my observation that Australia stands in an intermediate position between the U.S.A. and Holland.

It is not easy for any country to organise an age-group pro-

124

gramme on a national scale, so many factors such as finance, pool facilities, and distance, present a challenge. Nevertheless I am certain that age-group swimming on the same lines as in the U.S.A. is the key to competitive success. Each country must solve these problems in its own way.

23

Age-Group Testimonials from Parents, Doctors and Swimming Writers

IN DEFENCE OF AGE-GROUP SWIMMING
by Barbara Harvey (Arlington, Va.)

RIGHT after the 1960 Olympic Games, in which the United States swim teams were spectacularly successful, coaches, the public, and swimmers themselves, were loud in praise of the U.S. AAU'S age-group swim programme. Much of the credit for the success in Rome was given age-group swimming. Tokyo merely added an exclamation point to these statements. Age-group is not a one-shot Olympic deal.

In the years since, there has been an about-face in many quarters. A tendency to carp and criticize has become increasingly noted.

Is this criticism valid?

From the viewpoint of the original purpose of the age-group programme, the answer can be 'yes'. But from the perspective of what age-group has actually become, the answer differs. Originally, age-group was designed to provide controlled competition for youngsters interested in training but not yet ready for Junior and Senior open competition. It was to be a stepping stone. No one foresaw the enthusiastic response to the age-group programme. Thousands upon thousands upon thousands of youngsters flocked to it, and mostly for the pure fun and glory of it. To these ever increasing thousands, age-group swimming has become an end in itself. And this is precisely what many coaches object to. These coaches, and some other critics, feel that some able swimmers wear out their competitive lives in age-group contests, and never go on to full potential in national and international competition.

Age-group swimming can still be a stepping stone in the

126

bined committee of the National Education Association and the American Medical Association. The committee said that inter-scholastic athletic competition for girls should be limited to 'sports-days and play-days where mass participation is empha-sized'.

The book, which, as I write, is undergoing complete revision for a fourth edition, also recommended that 'all girls' athletic activities should be taught, coached, and refereed, by profes-sionally prepared women leaders, and should be divorced en-tirely from any inter-scholastic athletic contests for boys'.

DISAGREES WITH THEORY

Dr Barnes disagreed with this approach and dismissed argu-ments in defence of it – loss of femininity, fear of encouraging athletic professionalism in the girls, and the like – as 'tommyrot'.

Dr Barnes cited Yale and other university studies that showed a decline in the fitness of entering freshman, together with esti-mates that in many rural areas fewer than 20 per cent of the high-school students were getting any supervised physical educa-tion, and pointed out that these figures applied to boys.

'The girls' situation is worse,' he said.

'Consider, some schools have six to eight cheerleaders, maybe two to four majorettes; then there are twelve girls active for all four or five months out of the year. Look at the college situation, where there may be only three or four girls active, many colleges having no athletic programme for women students.'

Among the reasons for the neglect of physical education for girls, according to Dr Barnes, is the old-fashioned 'ladies-should-not-perspire' mentality of many physical educators.

'Unfortunately,' he said, 'this group has frequently controlled PTA groups, and has scared parents into believing that girls should not exert themselves.'

DECRIES UNFOUNDED FEARS

Dr Barnes said there are countless fears and beliefs concern-ing the dangers to women participating in athletics that are not founded on known facts.

'Physicians and coaches have asked if the running broad jump can cause harm to the reproductive potential of females,' he

131

said. 'The answer here, as in many other similar questions, is, physical education and athletics do not represent any significant hazard for the healthy female. Women are not the weaker sex in all respects.

'The illness rate is considerably higher among boys at most ages. Female superiority persists, as reflected by illness rates, and by the women's greater life expectancy. Our girls are not fragile packages that must be protected and coddled at all times – unless we make them so.'

Dr Barnes quoted Dr Gyula J. Erdelyi's study of 450 Hungarian female athletes (Medical Tribune, May 23, 1960), which 'revealed that sport participation does not delay the onset of menses and does not cause significant change in the menstrual cycle'.

'There is no clear-cut effect on dysmenorrhea and no deleterious results at all on subsequent pregnancy and labour among female athletes,' he added. 'Furthermore, participation in sports in early life apparently does not in any way alter the bony pelvis. There is considerable evidence that there is no consistent change in proficiency in a sport during various phases of the menstrual cycle, and it is generally agreed that a female athlete may compete in most sports at any time during her menstrual cycle.'

Aside from fears of physical injury, parents also worry about emotional disturbances caused by competition, Dr Barnes said.

'In a very long practice, I have never seen a child or an adolescent who, because of his competitiveness in sports, had become emotionally disturbed or mentally ill to such a degree as to have to consult a psychiatrist. Athletic girls are never the "weak and nervous" type we all hate to see and treat.'

Dr Barnes noted that athletics, and physical education, are part of the overall training of an individual, teaching him loyalty, comradeship, and a sense of responsibility towards the student body and the school. He expressed concern for future generations whose mothers lacked the opportunity to learn such attributes.

'A girl grows into womanhood, becomes a mother, having never played a team sport, does not understand the rules of most sports, and has no interest in athletic activities,' Dr Barnes said. 'Can this woman raise boys – or girls – who want to play?

This woman knows only that athletes get hurt. She feels that contact sports are senseless, and can see no value in them – so she forbids her son to play.'

'DAD IS TOO BUSY'

'Unfortunately, the boys of today seldom have a father to aid them in their growth to manhood. Dad is too busy, too ambitious, and "leaves the driving" to Mum. Many a boy has missed his one chance in life to be important because of a frail, non-athletically oriented mother.

'He may also have missed a chance to become a man.'

There is, however, some hope for the future in the new breed of female physical educator who does not feel strenuous exercise makes a girl less feminine, Dr Barnes said.

'The teachers who feel that stress and strain are unladylike are gradually being aged out of the picture. We are having a change in the attitude of parents, and family physicians, regarding the use of "medical" excuses to get Susie out of her gym class because she did not want to get her new bouffant hairdo messed up.

'Television has shown young girls that girls do compete in a variety of sports, and that it can be exciting and glamorous. Educators, slow to be sure, are gradually permitting girls to engage in more physical activities. The Olympic Games have shown that girl athletes do not necessarily develop figures like New York Giant tackles, that many foreign female athletes are quite attractive, and that men are attracted to the girl athlete.'

Amen, Doctor! We can go a long way towards changing the North American attitude about women athletes if we show the Olympic gymnastics films in our schools. The beauty, grace, and skill, of those girl gymnasts is such a superb example of physical beauty and femininity, it would make the opposition to physically fit womanhood sound ridiculous.

The Inches to Success

by Howard G. Woodward, Jr

This article is dedicated to thousands of parents, and their youngsters, in order that they might gain a greater insight into the dynamic functions of a swimming team, its coaches, and members. It's not written to discourage, but rather to encourage parent participation and point out what place each person – parent, coach, swimmer – has on the team.

Since Beth Kaufman initiated the Age-Group Swimming programme, experience has shown that conflicts between the parent-coach-swimmer have resulted in unnecessary heart-break. If some directive or method were followed by all involved, the unfortunate experience might easily be avoided.

How does it all start? Somewhere hidden deep in every youth is an infinitesimal spark, the desire to compete. All that need be done is to start that spark kindling and, bango!, the entire family is thrust helter-skelter into the competitive ranks. How does the spark get there? A geneticist will say that the major share of a swimmer's talent is due to heredity, that is, passed on to him from Mum and Dad. However, he must have an inherent desire to compete. It is something like spring fever, it runs in your blood. Maybe it is through the swim programme at the local 'Y', or the past summer's Junior Olympics, but all of a sudden your child is a Swimmer. From this moment on, the competitive sport of swimming becomes an integrated part of your child's life and, to him, it carries a great and powerful meaning.

Those parents who bear a keen interest in their child's physical, as well as moral growth, put their shoulders to the wheel and give their child, as well as the coach, a hand. People of this type, I am sorry to say, are in the minority. Today's Age-Group teams are large, and this calls for close teamwork on the part of the members and parents too. If a coach had this support, it would lighten his mental load, thus allowing him to use his skill to the best of his ability. Teamwork is a small word, but

134

it encompasses the parents, coaching staff, and swimmers alike, and its dividends are tremendous.

The parent is not a coach and, therefore, has no duties as a coach, but he does make an excellent spectator. The parents share a large part in the sport by providing guidance, assurance, encouragement, a well-balanced diet, and seeing that the child obtains the proper amount of sleep. They teach the child to observe and listen to the coach, and expose him to the fact that he fits into and is a needed part of the team.

Parents can form a council which can be coach's right-hand man, giving him the needed advice concerning his team and its evolution. Parents should be willing, when called upon by the coach, to lend a hand. From coast to coast one will find that a coach's major problem, which at first he says is swimmers, really is the parents' undermining of the child's confidence in himself. Only a minor portion of the parents know competitive swimming, and how to handle their child in it. Each time a parent scolds his child because he did not take first place, he smothers the competitive fire. At this point, the coach either loses a swimmer, or fights a harder battle to rebuild the child's confidence. Therefore, a parent's best advice before a race is, 'You do your very best. We'll be behind you all the way'. After the race is swum, and the victory has been decided, how about, 'You did your very best and we're proud of you.'?

It is a known fact that the parent has the duty of bringing his child up properly. Therefore, the child is the parent's responsibility. In the case of what I shall call extra-curricular activity – that in which the child becomes someone else's responsibility. – the parent turns his responsibilities of child care over to the person in charge of the activity. Here, swimming fits into this category. True, in a few exceptional cases, the parents know a good deal about competitive swimming, but when the child enters the world of swimming he becomes the coach's responsibility to the extent that it is his job to guide the child in the right channels towards the correct goal, as he sees fit. It is at this point that the parent should step into the background and give the coach a chance to prove himself, thus, bringing forth, as a result of his knowledge of the subject, the best swimmer he can develop.

A swimming-coach is a person who knows every angle of

the game. He has training and experience under his belt which both parents and swimmer lack. He, therefore, is designated to develop the swimmer to perform to the best of his ability. He uses his own techniques to insure supreme muscle co-ordination through the medium of regular practice sessions. Because he has a sound grasp of each of the strokes, and knows all the fine points, he is the coach. It is up to the coach to keep the spark of swimming alive and growing in each of his swimmers. His eye is trained to pick out the faults which determine the difference between a champion and a novice. Because the coach has these many qualities, he reserves the righ to run the training programme as a solo flight. It is for a reason similar to this that a mining engineer isn't a banker, and *vice versa*. It is the coach who gives the swimmer the needed confidence to stand quietly on the block before a race and also to be sure of himself.

A swimmer, be he a winner or not, gains a great deal by merely being a team member. He learns how to live with his fellow man, and that he is an essential link in the team. Clean competition and fellowship are rewards which in themselves can never be gained, created, or purchased for the price of the material award for winning a race. The swimmer is actually building for the future, and not just for that first place gold medal. Success as a competitor means practice and participation. It does not necessarily mean winning. In swimming, as in any sport, there is not a place for *prima donnas*, but there is plenty of room for those who are willing and ready to do their best. Success means meeting failure without being discouraged and then doing all that you can, as a swimmer, to improve yourself and achieve your goal.

The Age-Group Programme—A Physical Necessity

by J. V. Curran, M.D.

Dr J. V. Curran, M.D., has been associated with swimming for many years, and is closely associated with the Chuck Lee Swim Club, Everett, Washington. Believing that we are now

Trampoline exercises can help to keep swimmers of all ages in first-class condition

Two studies of a very young age-grouper

*approaching 'open season' on age-group parents and coaches,
we have asked Dr Curran to answer the age-group critics from
the standpoint of health.*

IN this age of automation, when all industry and business
may eventually boil down to 'push-buttons', man may have
to revert to some form of organized athletics to keep his body
in sufficient physical shape to survive the vigours and rigours of
the society in which he exists.

Recently, Dr Shane McCarthy, Chairman of the President's
Commission on the health needs of the nation, pointed out the
poor physical status of American youth. There have been many
other outspoken people in the field of health and welfare who
have been crying out against the babying of our young people.
The softness of their bodies, through failure of use during the
development years, has created a nation of young people who
are, in a word, 'softies'. These authorities continually point out
we do not have enough vigorous activity to develop our physical
vigour to the point where an individual will have such a good
body, that he will also be able to house an alert mind.

DEFINITE VALUE TO YOUTH

It is in this area that age-group swimming can be of definite
value to the youth of our nation. It would help to develop a
smooth, symmetrical body that will effect all the limbs and
musculature of the shoulders, back, arms, legs, and abdomen,
to their fullest potential without developing bulky, unsightly
muscles. This type of activity will place a sufficient amount of
stress on the respiratory and heart system. For in youths, it is
essential to life and to good health that sufficient activity of a
vigorous nature in the big-muscle area be done early in order
that heart-lung response to activity will be able to meet any
of the stresses later on in life.

It is at this point that we should offer age-group swimming
in order to increase the health status of our youth. This is the
only activity offered to all ages, and both sexes, from the tender
years right on through to adulthood. Moreover, certain dangers
in the body contact sports are not inherent in this swimming
programme.

The one facet of age-group swimming that is most important,

and often overlooked, is that it is the only outlet that is available in organized fashion, not only on a competitive basis, but in the development of physical vigour of the young ladies of our nation without the development of a bulky, heavy, musculature of which they are often not fond. There is very little of any activity available on a continuous basis to young females, particularly in the eight-and-under group, and on up through the teens.

WIDE VARIETY

The age-group swimming programme offers youth a wide variety of activities in the water that are a definite big-muscle activity. The strong body, the healthy lungs, and the good heart responses necessary to produce a swimmer, are, of course, to be found in any athletic endeavour. However, age-group swimming can be continued the year round, and the advantage of a continuous, vigorous programme is paramount.

The tremendous interest shown in age-group swimming, the fact that water has a tremendous fascination for youngsters who will play in it by the hour, can be channelled into development of physical vigour in our youth. Trained coaches give these young ones the same amount of play in the water, but it will be through planned training, resulting in a better developed body.

Most other types of activities, such as basketball, etc., are short term – four to six month periods of development – and then the activity ceases until another season rolls around. This is not an ideal method of development of one's physical vigour. People should have some type of big-muscle activity continuously the year around.

EASILY EXPLAINED

Consider some of the objections one encounters in respect to swimming. They are easily explained away. Notable is the chlorine-burning of the eyes which can be handled by the use of other types of water treatment, such as iodine. However, it has been my experience, as a physician and a swimming coach over the past 20 years, that I have seen no harmful effects from the use of chlorine other than the immediate discomfort. Another objection is that swimming produces ear infection. The ear infections that develop from water are the result of water passing into the nose, washing infectious material into the Eustachian tubes, and hence into the inner ear. There are two methods of handling this problem. Number one is to teach the swimmer to breathe correctly. Number two is to have him breathe more vigorously. Few swimmers vigorously exhale enough in the water and thus are unable to get sufficient amount of oxygen returning to their lungs and their efficiency is cut down, particularly in the lung recess. At the same time, the vigorous exhalation through the nose and mouth would clear the passages and prevent many of these infections that could be attributed to participation in water activities.

Properly controlled water treatment, with more intensive study of the water treatment systems of our country, could abolish these problems and make our age-group swimming programme that much better.

With millions swimming in the United States alone, it should be a 'must' programme for our chemical industry to research into water bacteriology, and treatment to find a new system and make the use of chlorine obsolete.

EMOTIONAL STABILITY

A criticism most paramount among people not closely associated with age-group swimming is the question of emotional stability of the young in a competitive activity. I feel they gain several things. The child acquires the feeling that he has a measure of skill in being able to swim better, faster, and hence safer. There is a certain assurance of self-satisfaction in being able to handle yourself better in water. Organization of an age-group swimming programme makes possible for him a wealth of supervised, organized programmes by a group of persons intensely interested in promoting swimming.

COMPETITIVE SWIMMING VITAL

In a learn-to-swim programme, competitive swimming is a definite part of learning to swim better. By this, I mean, that no beginning swimming programme is complete without some effort at attempting to initiate a person to swim farther, and faster, in order to be more proficient. Recently, the American Red Cross has adopted age-group swimming in its 'Learn-to-

Swim' to step up its life-saving programme. Age-group gives a youngster an opportunity to race under good conditions. He is prepared by adequate training programmes before competition as he works with his team-mates. This is of great value in teaching one to compete not only for himself and his team, but understanding the need for proper preparation.

Certain people will not participate in a competitive programme that includes only racing. This can be handled in an age-group swimming programme, with the inclusion of diving, water ballet and skin-diving. These also offer competition but of a varied nature.

CONCERTED PROGRAMME

There are persons who are gifted by early maturity and are outstanding with a minimum of effort. But, for the most part, those who have been able to succeed have had to take a concerted programme of activity that required self-denial as well as a singleness of purpose, and organization of their time and efforts. The calibre of swimming throughout the United States has improved tremendously since the age-group programme has got underway. The full impact of this is beginning to show now as almost all of America's present top-flight swimmers came out of, or are still in, the age-group programme. All of our age-group swimmers are not going to become Olympic or National champions, but they should be encouraged to develop themselves wholly and vigorously from a very early age . . . to develop their bodies and minds, to learn to accept defeat, taste victory, and to get along with their team-mates and fellow competitors and, lastly, to compete on a team basis, placing their team welfare on a higher plane than their own.

Finally, there is a definite asset in that it helps keep young people busy and off the streets. It will help reduce juvenile delinquency by utilizing healthfully any excessive free time of our young people.

HOLD AMERICAN FUTURE

Dr Adelbert Oberteuffer of Ohio State University, told physical educators they hold America's future in their hands. 'When all living – work and play – boils down to push-buttons,' he said, 'Man will have to revert to the physical education programme in order to keep his body fit.'

We must extend our physical education activities and encourage and develop further, age-group swimming programmes through the nation. Age-group swimming not only offers survival in the water, but survival for health, wealth, and happiness, in the future.

A Parent Looks at Age-Group Swimming
by Daniel Bernd

Daniel Bernd, Assistant Professor of English at San Fernando Valley State College, Northridge, California, is the father of two age-group swimmers, a boy 9, and a girl 13.

LIKE most parents, I suppose, we got into age-group swimming rather casually, without realizing at the time that we had got on the back of a tiger, that competitive swimming is the sport where the rule of all or nothing applies most rigidly. The hour spent at the Saturday morning swimming class has expanded to the daily work-out, the week-end contest, the all-encompassing family interest. The question arises: is it worth it? Does the child get enough out of swimming to justify the enormous expenditure of time and effort? Are the sacrifices of other activities justified? Each family must answer those questions for itself, of course. My own answers come out of my attempts to explain what we are doing to friends who cannot quite understand why we devote half of our lives to watching a bunch of kids churn up and down a swimming-pool. They can understand swimming, yes. Here, in Southern California, we all like to swim. But why competitive swimming?

Here are the answers I give, the reasons I have for claiming that swimming is the best of all possible sports:

1. Any child can do it. There is probably no other sport in which all children are created equal. Given good teaching, all children can learn to swim, and to swim well. Any

normal child can become a good competitive swimmer, if he wants to. There are naturals in swimming, of course, just as there are in any sport, but most easily in swimming can natural advantages be offset by intelligent instruction and hard work. The implications of the pioneer work of C. C. Fries and Matt Mann in teaching children how to swim have not yet been fully realized. Fries and Mann found that children can be taught to swim at a very early age (Fries taught his son Charles to swim before he could walk). Their work indicates the universality of the sport, for they found that once fear of the water is overcome (by some rather simple techniques), all children love the water, as naturally as ducks.

2. In swimming, the child can therefore easily see the relationship between work and results. In other sports, the phrase 'character-building' is too often a cliché without meaning, but in swimming there is a clear day-to-day discipline involved that teaches the child that he who works succeeds. In competitive swimming, if you work, you get better. If you don't work, you don't get better. Few things in life are that simple for children. The advantage here is that swimming is a sport, because it is fun, character is 'built' in a relatively painless fashion. We should be careful about claiming carry-over into other activities, but surely experience with hard, systematic work has obvious benefits that need no further justification. If our educational system has any main fault it is that we do not sufficiently encourage children to stretch themselves to the limits of their abilities. A competitive swimming team is an excellent vehicle for giving children a chance to find out how good they are – in their own terms.

3. Swimming is almost unique in that it gives the young age-grouper an absolute standard of his own performance. In what sport (other than track) can a young person know how good he is compared, not only with his peers, but also with world champions? The stop-watch gives a swimmer a means to measure his achievements by his own standards, against the standards of the best. In every race, in every work-out, he knows just how well he has done, how much he has improved. In other sports, he may know only whether he has won or lost. In swimming, he can tell just how well he played the game.

4. Swimming provides a blend of individual and co-operative effort that almost exactly reflects the major forces in American society. Our laws and customs stress the sanctity of the individual while, at the same time, our whole social structure depends upon co-operative group effort. In no other country does the term 'team' carry the weight it does in America. Note how swimming reflects this dual nature of our life much more accurately than football – a sport divided into lower and upper classes (the line and the backfield). Not so with swimming. In a relay race, each swimmer's contribution is as important and obvious as another's, yet it is the total effort that counts. Every swimmer who finds himself swimming some other stroke than his best because the team needs him in that slot is learning something about his society that he needs to know. Yet his effort is not submerged into the statistics of the won-lost column. The stop-watch precisely measures and recognizes his individual contribution to a team effort.

5. One of the major advantages of competitive swimming is that it has almost no professional possibilities. Professional competition among swimmers is not very likely. Consequently, swimming probably will remain an amateur sport, relatively free of the pressures of professionalism. Most of the people in swimming are in the sport because they love it, not because they are going to get rich at it. In few other sports are questions and problems so habitually resolved in terms of what is good for the kids, not in terms of what is good for the owners, the managers, or the ticket-sellers.

6. One not unimportant advantage of competitive swimming is that the novice associates with the champion in a manner denied to sports divided into rareful hierarchies of major and minor leagues. A Dick Nelson spends his Saturday mornings teaching young boys in a City Recreation Department beginning class. A Carolyn House chats with a young thirteen-year-old, scared at her first venture into a senior contest. Your child may be in the slow heat, and the national record holder in the fast heat, but at least they are in the same race. The camaraderie among swimmers of all classes and abilities, a devotion to the sport for its own sake, is a strong part of what we may term the ethos of swimming.

143

These then, are what I would term the major advantages of competitive swimming. The question for the parent becomes one of deciding how best his children can benefit from these advantages. One thing we parents have been told often enough : leave the coaching to the coaches. In all good sense, we would have to agree with this advice. It does the child no good to destroy his confidence in what he is doing by 'second guessing' his coach. And too many proud parents want their boy made into a national champion forthwith, this year, without stopping to consider the effect this kind of pressure may have on the child, his coach, or his team. The parent's place may well be in the home, not on the pool deck, as Rose Mary Dawson says.

Yet something should be said in defence of that monster, the interfering swimming club parent. In the first place, the age-grouper cannot be turned over to the coach like a college football player. The parent knows his child, his temperament, and his needs, in a way no coach can or should. The parent must co-operate with the coach but so must the coach co-operate with the parent. Let me put it this way : the parent has no right to interfere, but he has the right to be consulted. The age-grouper's training schedule, his strokes, the events he swims, are the parent's business. The coach should make the decisions, and the decisions should be respected, but so should the parents' right to know why. As a parent, I have no intention of telling our coach how to run his business, anymore than I would try to tell a doctor how to take out my appendix, but neither do I intend to abdicate my responsibility to help decide what is best for my children.

Because our children have decided for us that the best thing for them is competitive swimming, we will have to keep on pushing them when they need pushing, praising them when they need praising, doing that all-important job of getting them to the pool on time. In answering the question of why competitive swimming, we have come to the point of wondering, not why we do it, but rather, why doesn't everybody?

My Kid Can Lick Your Kid

by Daniel Bernd

(Valley State College, Northridge, Calif.)

WHEN I was a boy, we used to say, 'My Dad can lick your Dad!' Unfortunately, the parents of some swimming youngsters have twisted the boast to read, 'My kid can lick your kid!' In the world of age-group swimming we like to feel that we are above the infamous Little League parent who ruins his son's enjoyment of the game by getting his own ego too involved with the boy's batting average, yet I sometimes think that we aren't so much better after all. We have our own version, right at the pool-side.

It would be a dull world indeed if we could not gain vicarious satisfaction out of our children's accomplishments, but we must learn to draw the line between reasonable pride and unreasonable pressure. When I see a child crying because he didn't win, I ask myself whether he is bothered because of his failure to live up to his own expectations or because of his worry that his parents won't love him if he loses.

I am speaking primarily here of the younger age-groups. If a 12-year-old boy views every race as a mortal combat rather than an enjoyable contest, he is in for trouble. If a nine-year-old girl worries that she going to lose a friend if she beats her in a race, then she is taking a sport a lot more seriously than a nine-year-old ought to be taking anything.

There are some peculiar psychological hazards built into age-group swimming that we have to take account of it we expect our children to keep on swimming when they reach high-school and college. We cannot avoid some of the problems, but we can keep them from getting out of hand. For example, there is the trauma of changing age-groups. After the youngster works his way up the ladder for two years, his birthday present is a shove back down into the pack. After placing consistently, it is difficult for an age-grouper to keep his perspective when he finds all those children in front of him again. There are only a few swimmers who manage to stay in front on changing age-groups. This is the time the age-grouper needs support – not complaints like 'Why did you let Johnny beat you?' He has to

145

learn to expect, and accept, a let-down from the heady atmosphere of medal-winning. It is up to the parent to be helpful and encouraging at this point, not only to their own children, but to other children too.

Another hazard is what I would call the top-gun psychology. As soon as a youngster begins 'to place', the other swimmers naturally begin to point towards beating him – a boy swims not only against time but also against other boys. There is nothing wrong with this *per se*, so long as it is kept within bounds. For example, my own son's ambition was to beat, just once, in one race, the best all-round swimmer in his age-group. He finally managed it (by judge's decision) but he did not lose the boy's friendship thereby, nor did his parents stop speaking to us. We were not carrying on a personal vendetta against a youngster who was so presumptuous as to swim faster than our son. The point is that it is bad sportsmanship to let a young swimmer feel the psychological pressure from adults who have zeroed in on him as the one young Georgie has to beat or the week-end is ruined. To the losers, the winning age-grouper ought to be a standard of excellence, not a personal enemy.

I do not mind if the children play the old game of 'psych-out' amongst themselves. In fact, I always rather enjoy eavesdropping on the ready bench, listening to them tell lies to each other about their times. But I am not going to play that game myself. Of course, the boys know that I would rather see my son win than lose, but I hope that I do not give him any extra advantage by trying to wage psychological warfare against his rivals. I am afraid I do not have much but contempt for the occasional adult who upsets a child by letting him 'overhear' hostile and critical remarks.

The amount and kind of pressure to put on a youngster is the parents' own business, of course. I have my own opinion of parents who put little children on an Olympian's training schedule, but that is ultimately their business, not mine. What is my business, however, is the kind of atmosphere created in a sport I want my children to continue in by people who take it too seriously. Swimming is not a model of life, except in a very general sense. A boy can be a third-rate swimmer and still be a first-rate boy. There are great values in the sport for all swimmers as long as they do not have to contend with over-zealous parents who have their egoes locked into the five best-time rating.

As for myself, I have never won a race in my life. I hope that I never forget that it is my children doing the racing, not me.

Swimming and Ears

by Hugh O. Barber, M.D. F.R.C.S.

(Department of Otolaryngology, University of Toronto)

The expression 'out on your ear' is no joke to age-group swim-ming coaches who have had their best team efforts wrecked by long absenteeism due to 'swimmer's ear'. Age-Group swimming clubs do not have the advantage of a team physician or school doctor so this matter should be discussed before it arises at an early parents' meeting. The family physician must be aware of his swimmer's problems as a swimmer, before making decisions on the swimmer's problems as a patient. The author is an ear specialist who also happens to be the president of a swimming club and the father of two age-group swimmers.

At the outset, I must emphasize that nobody should engage in competitive swimming if they have a perforation of the ear-drum, as serious ear disease may result. When you have ear trouble you should see a doctor, but the doctor should be made aware of your problems as a swimmer. The standard practice of the pampered swimmer saying, 'it hurts', and the doctor saying, 'stay out of the water three weeks', will not work out if you are training for a swimming contest. Three weeks out of the water may wreck your swimming, and you must be sure your doctor understands this, and that your parents understand this, and that they understand that swimming is very important to the swimmer. A doctor sympathetic to this will evaluate things in a different light and keep you out of the water only if it is absolutely necessary to your health. Besides, if your ear trouble is what a swimmer's ear trouble usually is, three weeks out of the water will not cure it, nor will three weeks in the water cause any serious or lasting damage. Let me explain :

147

One of the commonest health problems that swimmers encounter is external otitis, and inflammation of the ear channel and outer surface of the drum. The symptoms are itching, irritation, and periodic ear-ache, sometimes discharge, and occasionally severe pain in the ear. This disorder, though minor, is an occupational hazard in swimming, in the same way that nodules of the vocal cords bedevil the singer. Swimmers will have these ear-aches periodically until they finally quit swimming so they must learn to live with them. This is part of the price they pay to be champions and not one champion got there without learning to live with some small pain.

The basic cause of the trouble is frequently repeated wetting of the canal skin, and it really does not matter if the water is fresh or salt, pure or dirty, swimming-pool or shower. Skin that is normally tough and dry becomes gradually softened; its outer layers get mushy and are cast off in softened scales or flakes which accumulate in the canal. Germs that normally inhabit skin may then be able to invade the ear passage, causing varying degrees of infection.

If all this sounds worrisome, it need not. I think swimmers (and parents) should remember that swimmer's ear virtually never produces serious effects in terms of important illness, provided the skin is basically healthy to start with. When swimming days are over, the skin of the ear reverts to normal, unscarred by its former troubles.

Surely it is a matter of priorities. To me, and speaking as a parent of two eager swimmers, the advantages of competitive swimming, social, disciplinary and health, far outweigh the nuisance of the ear that itches and aches a bit. I rarely keep a serious swimmer out of the water for this diagnosis.

Even so, a number of things can be done to minimize the condition. I believe that bathing-caps and especially ear-plugs, should never be used. Caps invariably leak and also may prevent water already in the ear from draining out. Plugs tend to rub and injure already softened skin, hence promote infection. Here are some suggestions for care of swimmer's ear that may be helpful:

1. After practice, make sure that water in each ear has drained out – shake head, kick leg etc., but do not dig at your ears.
2. Then put a few drops of 65–70% ethyl alcohol in each

ear. Your doctor can give you a prescription for this. Otherwise, use ordinary rubbing alcohol. These drops toughen and dry the ear skin. They may sting for a minute or so.

3. In the uncommon event that severe pain and swelling occurs, a thin ear drop containing a steriod drug (cortisone-like agent) and antibiotic is effective in reducing the inflammation. Pain-killing drugs (aspirin, codeine) should be used as required. It may be necessary in unusual cases to avoid swimming for several days, but not several weeks, until the worst of the storm has passed.

4. Remember that swimming is more important than minor ear troubles. Be brave!

Conclusions

Age-group Swimming may or may not be the answer to your Olympic development problems in other countries, and in other sports, but it certainly has been a success story in the U.S.A. That this success was partially due to good luck is obvious from the book you have just read. No one guessed what age-group's scope might be back in 1948, when first proposed, and in 1952 when first acted upon as a working programme. The very size of the programme brought on a variety of problems, most of which have been solved. Frank discussion of these problems in this book is supposed to help you on a local, state, national, or international level decided what there is about U.S. Age-Group Swimming that can key your programmes in swimming and in other sports. Perhaps we have been too harsh in dramatizing our problems since the success of age-group as a swimming programme has been irrefutable. Criticism is engendered by the vision that this programme has meant and can mean much more than swimming success. For the U.S., and perhaps for much of the world, the success of age-group swimming establishes a need that youth craves to be satisfied through competitive sports. Our mission is not so much to sell age-group swimming as a programme for Olympic success as to sell it as a blueprint for teenage needs in a racing world. The demands made on youth through unconditional commitment to age-group swimming are training for adult life where the discipline learned in a swimming-pool can help create a stronger individual to help make a better society.

The biggest thrill I got at the Olympic Games was seeing all those athletes, representing many flags, in peaceful competition. They were human beings first, athletes second, and nationalists third. It was a United Nations in action, and the competition was sportsmanship, the golden rule in action. Age-Group Swimming is one method of reaching hundreds of thousands of youngsters and their parents with this Golden Rule in action.

Appendix I

Official U.S. AAU Age-Group Swimming and Diving Rules

A. SWIMMING

1. Associations may have age-group competition consisting of four age groups as follows: 10 and under, 11-12 years, 13-14 years and 15-17 years. Times may be submitted for Age-Group record and five best times recognition for an Age-Group swimmer participating in any sanctioned Junior and Senior AAU competition, except relays.

2. No record attempt time trials are acceptable in age-group swimming. All records must be made in actual sanctioned competitive meets. Performance made in AAU Junior Olympic competition may not be submitted for National Age-Group tabulation.

3. The eligibility of a participant for a particular age-group will be determined by his date of birth in his respective age-group. Age on the first day of the meet shall govern for the full-meet. Participants must swim in their respective age brackets. Misrepresentations of age will draw a suspension for three months.

4. The eligibility to participate shall be determined by the age and the participant shall not be restricted from the age-group competition by having won an Association Championship, a National Championship, Pan American Championship or an Olympic Championship.

5. No contestant, in any one day, may compete in more than three events, exclusive of relays.

6. An Age-Group Chairman and committee shall be appointed from the District Associations.

7. The five (5) best times nationally in each age group shall be published for 20-yard course, short course and long course. Records to be forwarded not later than Sept. 15th of each year to the National Age-Group Chairman. Each association is responsible for reporting the five best times made in its association area only, even though the times were made by swimmers from other associations.

151

8. National AAU Age-Group champions as determined from the tabulated national results will be awarded official national emblems of a standard design, as adopted by the AAU and bearing the words 'A.A.U. Age-Group'. (Note: The national awards will be furnished without charge.)

9. AAU Swimming Rules to govern all Age-Group competition.

10. Awards for Age-Group events may not exceed a cost of $2.00 per swimmer for 1st place, $1.50 per swimmer for 2nd place, or $1.00 per swimmer for each place from 3rd through 8th. Awards for places beyond 8th are not allowed. Team Championship awards may not exceed a cost of $15.00. Individual high point awards may not exceed a cost of $2.00.

11. No pennant finish shall be allowed in an Age-Group meet.

12. THE EVENTS:

(10 Years and under)
20 YARD COURSE
40-100 yds Freestyle
40-100 yds Backstroke
40-100 yds Breaststroke
40-100 yds Butterfly
80-160 yds Ind. Medley
160 yds Medley Relay
160 yds Freestyle Relay

SHORT COURSE (25 yds up to 50 yds)
50-100 yds or mtrs Freestyle
50-100 yds or mtrs Backstroke
50-100 yds or mtrs Breaststroke
50-100 yds or mtrs Butterfly
100-200 yds or mtrs Ind. Medley
200 yds or mtrs Medley Relay
200 yds or mtrs Freestyle Relay

LONG COURSE (50 yds and up)
50-55-100-110 yds or 50-100 mtrs Freestyle
50-55-100-110 yds or 50-100 mtrs Backstroke
50-55-100-110 yds or 50-100 mtrs Breaststroke
50-55-100-110 yds or 50-100 mtrs Butterfly

152

The Fuerto Rico Swimming Association team which placed first in the Central American Age-Group Meet at El Salvador in 1962. Mrs Dawson and her father Matt Mann, helped in the preliminary training of this team, but they are not necessarily in favour of age-groupers going on long overseas trips

Many swim coaches use supplementary sports as well as supplementary exercises. Games help to keep age-group swimmers active, build up leg strength and improve cardio-vascular efficiency

200-220 yds or 200 mtrs Individual Medley
200-220 yds or 200 mtrs Medley Relay
200-220 yds or 200 mtrs Freestyle Relay
  (*11-12 Years*)

20 YARD COURSE
40-100-200 yds Freestyle
40-100 yds Backstroke
40-100 yds Breaststroke
40-100 yds Butterfly
160 yds Individual Medley
160 yds Medley Relay
160 yds Freestyle Relay
400 yds Medley Relay
400 yds Freestyle Relay

SHORT COURSE (25 yds up to 50 yds)
50-100-200 yds or mtrs Freestyle
50-100 yds or mtrs Breaststroke
50-100 yds or mtrs Butterfly
200 yds or mtrs Ind. Medley
200 yds or mtrs Medley Relay
50-100 yds or mtrs Backstroke
200 yds or mtrs Freestyle Relay
400 yds or mtrs Medley Relay
400 yds or mtrs Freestyle Relay

LONG COURSE (50 yds and up)
50-55-100-110-200-220 yds or 50-100-200 mtrs Freestyle
50-55-100-110 yds or 50-100 mtrs Backstroke
50-55-100-110 yds or 50-100 mtrs Breaststroke
50-55-100-110 yds or 50-100 mtrs Butterfly
200-220 yds or 200 mtrs Individual Medley
200-220 yds or 200 mtrs Medley Relay
200-220 yds or 200 mtrs Freestyle Relay
400-440 yds or 400 mtrs Medley Relay
400-440 yds or 400 mtrs Freestyle Relay

  (*13-14 Years*)
20 YARD COURSE
40-100-200-400 yds Freestyle
100-200 yds Backstroke

153

100-200 yds Breaststroke
100-200 yds Butterfly
160 yds Individual Medley
160 yds Medley Relay
160 yds Freestyle Relay
400 yds Medley Relay
400 yds Freestyle Relay

SHORT COURSE (25 yds up to 50 yds)
50-100-200-400 yds or mtrs Freestyle
100-200 yds or mtrs Backstroke
100-200 yds or mtrs Breaststroke
100-200 yds or mtrs Butterfly
200 yds or mtrs Individual Medley
200 yds or mtrs Medley Relay
200 yds or mtrs Freestyle Relay
400 yds or mtrs Medley Relay
400 yds or mtrs Freestyle Relay

LONG COURSE (50 yds and up)
50-55-100-110-200-220-400-440 yds or 50-100-200-400 mtrs
    Freestyle.
100-110-200-220 yds or 100-200 mtrs Backstroke
100-110-200-220 yds or 100-200 mtrs Breaststroke
100-110-200-220 yds or 100-200 mtrs Butterfly
200-220 yds or 200 mtrs Individual Medley
200-220 yds or 200 mtrs Medley Relay
200-220 yds or 200 mtrs Freestyle Relay
400-440 yds or 400 mtrs Medley Relay
400-440 yds or 400 mtrs Freestyle Relay

(15-16-17 Years)
20 YARD COURSE
GIRLS
40-100-220-500 yds Freestyle
100-200 yds Backstroke
100-220 yds Breaststroke
100-200 yds Butterfly
160-400 yds Ind. Medley
160-400 yds Medley Relay
160-400 yds Freestyle Relay

154

BOYS

40-100-200-500 yds Freestyle
100-200 yds Backstroke
100-200 yds Breaststroke
100-200 yds Butterfly
160-400 yds Ind. Medley
160-400 yds Medley Relay
160-400 yds Freestyle Relay

SHORT COURSE (25 yds up to 50 yds)

GIRLS

50-100-250-500 yds or 50-100-200-400 mtrs Freestyle
100-200 yds or mtrs Backstroke
100-250 yds or 100-200 mtrs Breaststroke
200-400 yds or mtrs Ind. Medley
200-400 yds or mtrs Medley Relay
200-400 yds or mtrs Freestyle Relay

BOYS

50-100-200-500 yds or 50-100-200-400 mtrs Freestyle
100-200 yds or mtrs Backstroke
100-200 yds or mtrs Breaststroke
200-400 yds or mtrs Ind. Medley
200-400 yds or mtrs Medley Relay
200-400 yds or mtrs Freestyle Relay

LONG COURSE (50 yds and up)

GIRLS

50-55-100-110-220-250-440-500 yds or 50-100-200-400 mtrs
    Freestyle
100-110-200-220 yds or 100-200 mtrs Backstroke
100-110-220-250 yds or 100-200 mtrs Breaststroke
100-110-200-220 yds or 100-200 mtrs Butterfly
200-220-400-440 yds or 200-400 mtrs Ind. Medley
200-220-400-440 yds or 200-400 mtrs Medley Relay
200-220-400-440 yds or 200-400 mtrs Freestyle Relay

BOYS

50-55-100-110-200-220-440-500 yds or 50-100-200-400 mtrs
    Freestyle
100-110-200-220 yds or 100-200 mtrs Backstroke
100-110-200-220 yds or 100-200 mtrs Breaststroke

155

100-110-200-220 yds or 100-200 mtrs Butterfly
200-220-400-440 yds or 200-400 mtrs Ind. Medley
200-220-400-440 yds or 200-400 mtrs Medley Relay
200-220-400-440 yds or 200-400 mtrs Freestyle Relay

Special Events: 17 and under
Long Distance, Team and Individual
Water Polo (Hard Ball)
Synchronized Swimming

B. DIVING

1. Age-group diving rules shall be consistent with senior diving rules except as specified below:

The diving referee has the authority to eliminate any dive if, in his opinion, circumstances exist which might endanger the competitors.

2. Each A.A.U. district association shall submit the name of its best diver in each age-group (boy and girl) to the national age-group diving chairman for recognition. This record must be received on or before September 15th and must be certified on the correct forms. Selection of the divers will be left to the discretion of each district association.

3. Five (5) Basic Dives:
    Front Dive (any position) Book degree of difficulty
    Back Dive (any position) Book degree of difficulty
    Inward Dive (any position) Book degree of difficulty
    $\frac{1}{2}$ Twist Fwd. (any position) Book degree of difficulty
    Reverse Dive (any position) Book degree of difficulty

4. A diver may eliminate any required dive and take zero on the dive, without prejudice, and remain in the contest. (This will provide a contest for all skill levels of competition. It will eliminate the danger of trying dives without preparation and will create a desire and need for young divers to learn all five required dives.) All dives must be listed in the official A.A.U. Swimming Handbook.

5. *10 and Under*—One (1) metre springboard diving:
    The five (5) required dives and one (1) optional, with book degree of difficulty.

156

6. *11-12 years*—One (1) metre and three (3) metre spring-board diving:

> The five (5) required dives and three (3) optional, with book degree of difficulty.

7. *13-14 years*—One (1) metre and three (3) metre spring-board diving:

> The five (5) required dives and five (5) optional, with book degree of difficulty.

8. *15-16-17 years*—One (1) metre and three (3) metre spring-board diving:

> The five (5) required dives and five (5) optional, with book degree of difficulty.

9. Platform diving for 12 years and over. Maximum height of platform, 5 metres, with water depth in accord with A.A.U. handbook. The first five dives shall be chosen one each from any five tables, and the sixth shall be chosen from any of the six tables. No dive may be repeated.

10. *All Age-Group*—None of the required dives may be repeated as an optional dive. All dives of the same number, whether in layout, pike or tuck position are to be considered as the same dive. Optional dives must be from different groups.

Appendix 11

Conversion Table for Sprint Distances

It is important for an age-group coach that he be able to tell what his swimmer should be able to do by projecting times – that an 11.2 25yd freestyler should be able to do 102.5 for 100 mtrs or 110 yds.

The following table is for use in English speaking countries where it is necessary to convert metres to feet and then to yards and vice versa—

50 mtrs equals	...	...	...	...	164.04 ft
60 mtrs equals	...	...	...	...	196.86 ft
100 mtrs equals	...	...	...	...	328.1 ft
200 mtrs equals	...	...	...	...	656.2 ft
300 mtrs equals	...	...	...	...	984.3 ft
400 mtrs equals	...	...	...	...	1,312.4 ft
500 mtrs equals	...	...	...	...	1,640.5 ft
600 mtrs equals	...	...	...	...	1,968.6 ft
800 mtrs equals	...	...	...	...	2,624.7 ft
1,000 mtrs equals	...	...	...	...	3,280.9 ft
1,500 mtrs equals	...	...	...	...	4,921.3 ft

DISTANCE IN YARDS

25	30	33⅓	40	44	50	55	60	66⅔	80	90	100	110
11.2	13.9	15.6	19.3	21.6	25.0	28.0	30.9	35.0	43.2	49.6	56	62.5
11.6	14.4	16.2	20.0	22.4	25.9	29.0	32.1	36.3	44.8	51.3	58	64.8
12.0	14.9	16.8	20.7	23.2	26.8	30.0	33.2	37.5	46.3	53.1	60	67.0
12.4	15.4	17.3	21.4	23.9	27.7	31.0	34.3	38.8	47.8	54.9	62	69.2
12.8	15.9	17.9	22.1	24.7	28.6	32.0	35.4	40.0	49.4	56.6	64	71.5
13.2	16.4	18.4	22.8	25.5	29.5	33.0	36.5	41.3	50.9	58.4	66	73.7
13.6	16.9	19.0	23.5	26.3	30.4	34.0	37.6	42.5	52.5	60.2	68	75.9
14.0	17.4	19.6	24.1	27.0	31.3	35.0	38.7	43.8	54.0	61.9	70	78.2
14.4	17.9	20.1	24.8	27.8	32.2	36.0	39.8	45.0	55.6	63.7	72	80.4
14.8	18.4	20.7	25.5	28.6	33.0	37.0	40.9	46.3	57.1	65.5	74	82.6
15.2	18.9	21.2	26.2	29.4	33.9	38.0	42.0	47.5	58.7	67.4	76	84.9
15.6	19.4	21.8	26.9	30.1	34.8	39.0	43.1	48.8	60.2	69.0	78	87.1
16.0	19.9	22.3	27.6	30.9	35.7	40.0	44.2	50.0	61.7	70.8	80	89.3
16.4	20.4	22.9	28.3	31.7	36.6	41.0	45.3	51.3	63.3	72.6	82	91.6
16.8	20.8	23.5	29.0	32.4	37.5	42.0	46.4	52.5	64.8	74.3	84	93.8
17.2	21.3	24.0	29.7	33.2	38.4	43.0	47.5	53.8	66.4	76.1	86	96.0
17.6	21.8	24.6	30.3	34.0	39.3	44.0	48.6	55.0	67.9	77.9	88	98.3
18.0	22.3	25.1	31.0	34.8	40.2	45.0	49.7	56.3	69.5	79.6	90	100.5
18.4	22.8	25.7	31.7	35.5	41.1	46.0	50.8	57.5	71.0	81.4	92	102.7
18.8	23.3	26.3	32.4	36.3	42.0	47.0	51.9	58.8	72.5	83.2	94	105.0
19.2	23.8	26.8	33.1	37.1	42.9	48.0	53.1	60.0	74.1	84.9	96	107.2

development of the potential champion. But more important, for every potential champion *hypothetically* worn out in age-group swimming, there are thousands upon thousands of youngsters who have enjoyed and benefitted from the sport.

So there are 'hardware collectors' encouraged by the always growing number of age-group meets? I do not object to that, providing each swimmer – and just as important, each parent – keeps perspective. For every medal that your child or mine may win in a contest at Podunk or Wokkington Falls, hundreds of medals are going the same day to other youngsters competing in other localities. Just do not over-estimate the importance of a medal won, or a time swum, by a ten-year-old. He or she is, after all, just one of many, many fish in the big age-group pond.

So, despite the original intent, or the regrets of coaches, age-group has become a sport in itself. It serves far greater numbers than ever before were served by swimming. And these numbers, in this era of worry over physical fitness, are getting an invaluable physical training.

Look how colleges have profited from this intense interest on the part of the 10- through 17-year-olds. Before the age-group programme, 'varsity swimming was a minor sport. Competitors came mainly from spotty scholastic swimming. Covering 44 AAU Associations, the age-group sport has produced a flood of boys wanting top swimming with their education. Instead of there being two or three swimming powers among the colleges, (Michigan, Ohio State and Yale), as in the past, the lists show champions now emerging from many schools There are so many boys coming from age-group swimming into the colleges, they are naturally spread out among many schools.

And the girls? Here is heard the most frequent complaint of all, i.e. the girl champions are getting younger and younger and are not lasting long at the top. This is bad?

Certainly there has been no sacrifice of quality. Each year's crop of records show times getting better in every stroke. To me, the quantity and turnover seems something to cheer about, not deplore. The girl swimmer, the girl athlete in general, has not found encouragement or available training in *any* athletic competition. Age-group provides the chance for girls to compete. And that girls seize this chance, that girls love athletic competi-

127

tion, is proved by the fact that more are attracted to age-group swimming every year, and new names constantly appear in the list of champions and record-breakers. The girls, young as they are, are swimming times undreamed of a few years ago, loving every bit of it and asking for more.

Let us accept age-group swimming for what is is, not for what it was intended to be. It grew out of its original frame to become an entirely new sports programme attracting more athletes than any other sport. Let's encourage these young athletes, and give them the programme they so obviously enjoy to the benefit of all.

WHAT MAKES AN AGE-GROUP SWIMMER DIFFERENT?
By Betty Johnson

A short time ago, after a crew of swimmers had left our home from a party, I was asked by a friend if I minded having all 'those kids' at our house. I was verbally chastised for my reply and in retrospect, I can realize now that my answer sounded quite biased and possibly somewhat pompous, and for that sound reason alone, I suppose I should have used a bit more diplomacy instead of outright bluntness, for my answer was, 'no, I don't object to "those kids," they're different from the others.' I was immediately asked, 'What do you mean, they're different. They're still young people aren't they? Surely swimmers are no more unique than any other crowd, so why do you say this?'

With that I began my defence. That, of course, was not my first nor probably last dissertation concerning the subject, so to conserve my energies for the more complex things of life, I would now like to state my case for the swimmers. I am not directing this article to interested parents, dedicated coaches or enthusiastic supporters of the programme, but I am directing it to school teachers, part time psuedo coaches, and to shallow minded adults who argue that we're turning our children and teenagers into swimming freaks. I am also directing this to small cliques who find nothing better to do than gossip about our ideals, our coach, and in many instances, our swimmers.

Now let's take a look at our swimmers and while we are at it, let's take a look at the other side of the coin also.

There's one very important factor that I do not think many

people are aware of today. So much has been written in the past few years about togetherness . . . fine, wonderful, but where do you draw the line? I remember growing up trying to emulate my parents, but somehow I find the role has been reversed today. Not so with the swimmer! He already has his set of values and it is not to see if he can grow a better tomato plant than mama or fly a higher kite than papa. He is doing something his parents cannot do and he is getting recognition and respect from his peers and elders because he has earned it. Our boys don't have to smoke and slash tyres in the seventh grade, and our girls don't have to wear scared hair and clothes so tight that breathing becomes hazardous. I will tell you one thing though, the hoods of this world respect him and her along with the rest of the kids who are otherwise leading very conforming lives. This gives our swimmers self respect and purpose, and this is one primary reason they're different.

We at Patton, belong to an unique organization and perhaps that is another reason our kids are different. Not one of our swimmers is a social snob. Sure, Joe Doke's family may have more money than John Doe's family, but so what? Money does not cut your time down nor lack of money keep you from becoming a champion. The only thing at Patton that money is, is a medium of exchange and 'amen' for that.

Not so, however, in the outside world. Our kids have already learned an important lesson in values. Keeping up with the Jones family is relatively unimportant to our kids. It is who is ahead at the hundred that counts or who is working the hardest to covet first place. They know it isn't a new dress or a new sports jacket that gives them self respect and recognition. It's work – hard work! Question – how many adults have learned this lesson?

Many people also feel our girls live very spartan lives, that dances, shows, and boys are out of the question for our gals. This also is another foible that belongs in the fairy tale classification. Not one of our girls is excluded from the so-called normal social graces. They have parties and activities when desired, but it's not an all consuming occupation. Popularity in the swimming world does not depend on dancing, but not one of our girls needs to take a back seat to the non-swimmer in high school or junior high. How many girls in the non-swimmer classification can travel, meet, be with, and compete against champions from all over the country. Most teen dances sound rather shallow and uninteresting in comparison, and a show could never equal an out of town swimming meet. All of these things have their place in growing up, but they certainly do not become first and foremost within the lives of our girls. This particular thought is directed at our girls, but I am sure it is another reason why swimmers are different.

It is so easy for small clubs to debase us because they simply do not speak the same language nor seek the same values. Competition is only a dual meet, meant to be fun, and not taken with too much seriousness or intent of purpose. Competition is much more than that. It is dedication to ideals, to elders who profess these ideals, and to coaches who fully realize the direction a champion wants to travel. Not every swimmer can become a champion, but ever swimmer can have the opportunity to try. The road is the same whether there's a pot of gold at the end or not, for the road is an ideal, a value, and a challenge. That is why swimmers are different.

Vigorous Athletics for Girls Defended
As Healthy Activity
by Dr Frank E. Barnes, Jr (Smithfield, N.C.)

THE opinion that girls can take part in vigorous competition without deleterious effects to their health was expressed here by Dr Frank E. Barnes, Jr, chairman of the school health committee of the North Carolina Medical Society.

Complaining that many educators still believe that girls' sporting activities should be limited to 'cheerleading' and 'prancing as drum majorettes', Dr Barnes said: 'It has been proved time and again that the healthy, happy, physically fit girl does better in school, is better adjusted in society, has more self-confidence, and tends to adjust to married life more easily.'

Dr Barnes took issue with the third edition of *Suggested School Health Policies* (published in 1956), prepared by a com-